Can Christianity Cure
OBSESSIVE-
COMPULSIVE
DISORDER?

Can Christianity Cure
OBSESSIVE-COMPULSIVE DISORDER?

A Psychiatrist Explores the Role of Faith in Treatment

IAN OSBORN, MD

BrazosPress

a division of Baker Publishing Group
Grand Rapids, Michigan

Bl. Brazos ⁴/₀₈ 17.99

Published by Brazos Press
a division of Baker Publishing Group
P.O. Box 6287, Grand Rapids, MI 49516-6287
www.brazospress.com

Printed in the United States of America

Library of Congress Cataloging-in-Publication Data
Osborn, Ian, 1946–
    Can Christianity cure obsessive-compulsive disorder? : a psychiatrist explores the role of faith in treatment / Ian Osborn.
      p.   cm.
    Includes bibliographical references.
    ISBN 978-1-58743-206-4 (pbk.)
    1. Obsessive-compulsive disorder—Religious aspects—Christianity.
2. Psychiatry and religion. I. Title.
    [DNLM: 1. Luther, Martin, 1483–1546. 2. Bunyan, John, 1628–1688.
3. Teresa, of Avila, Saint, 1515–1582. 4. Obsessive-Compulsive Disorder—therapy—Biography. 5. Christianity—psychology—Biography. 6. Famous Persons—Biography. 7. Obsessive-Compulsive Disorder—psychology—Biography. 8. Religion and Psychology—Biography. WZ 313 081c 2008]
    RC533.0827 2008
    616.85′227—dc22
                                             2007035431

Contents

Prologue
My Search

When I was in medical training, I suffered from obsessive-compulsive disorder. Irrational thoughts would jump into my mind and cause panic. I might be resting comfortably in my apartment, reading or watching television, when from out of the blue would come the startling image of my eye being poked out with a needle, a knife, or a scalpel. A sudden, piercing discomfort would lead me to rub my eye again and again.

At other times, I would be driving peacefully along a highway when I'd suddenly see my car swerving out of control and crashing into an oncoming truck. In vivid detail, I would see myself thrown through the windshield and scraped along the car hood, my nose shearing off, blood spattering everywhere.

To ease the sharp discomfort caused by these images, I would have to come up with a counterthought, a restorative image. I would replay the car-accident obsession, for instance, over and over in my mind, frame by frame, but in reverse order.

Fortunately, these mental intruders rarely struck when I was engaged in important activities such as studying or seeing patients. All in all, I was getting by. I was not, therefore, inclined to see a psychotherapist. If I did, I figured, I would be prescribed lengthy sessions of psychoanalysis, aimed at uncovering something buried in my unconscious. I feared that such treatment might make my condition even worse. Indeed, back then, therapy for anxiety disorders was widely considered to be a long-term process, and often futile. One expert had gone so far as to conclude, "Most of us are agreed that the treatment of obsessional states is one of the most difficult tasks confronting the psychiatrist, and many of us consider it hopeless."[1] So, I just plodded along, putting up with my symptoms.

As I reflected one day on my troublesome thoughts, I came to consider that perhaps what I needed was an entirely new perspective, a spiritual grounding. This idea took hold, and I felt a mounting sense of excitement. Since my background was Christian—my grandfather had been a minister, and I was baptized and confirmed as a Methodist—I thought I might find an answer there. I began to study Christianity seriously, something I had never done before. I remember sitting on the windowsill of my dorm room through many a long night, watching and praying until the quiet Pennsylvania countryside awakened to another dawn. Could Christianity cure these troublesome thoughts? I wondered.

For a couple of months, my search remained both invigorating and compatible with medical studies. Then it took on a compulsive and driven quality of its own. First came the nagging sense that I needed to work harder at my quest, to commit more time to it. Then a powerful urge to find an answer at any cost. Soon I found myself meditating, praying, and reciting Bible verses throughout the day. I stopped going to lectures. I failed a pharmacology test, and the head of that department, until then an aloof figure with whom I had never exchanged a word, took me aside and voiced a touching concern about my health. Friends, too, inquired about my well-being. At last I was shaken to the realization that my religious search had turned into an even greater problem than the one I had hoped to cure. The whole episode culminated in the most embarrassing moment of my life.

I decided that if God was real and was ever going to help me, now was the time. No more waiting. Perhaps, I reasoned, what was necessary was an act of submission, something that would demonstrate that I possessed what Judeo-Christian writers called "faith." One morning before dawn, I drove out into the rich farmland that surrounded the medical school. I climbed a fence and walked into a grassy field. There, I took off every stitch of my clothing, lay down on the cold earth, and looked up to the heavens, prepared to wait for God to show himself. Before the clouds could part, however, an anxiety attack the likes of which I had never experienced pierced me like a lightning bolt. I was sure the police would drive by and discover me, and I'd be kicked out of medical school forever! I threw on my clothes and hightailed it out of there, never looking back.

This incident, in all its apparent craziness, so unnerved me that I resolved to stop my spiritual search at once and pour myself into my studies. Fortunately, this tactic worked well enough to see me through. Then, when the stresses of medical school were over, I entered one of the most exciting times of my life, as a medical intern, and tormenting ideas ceased to be a major problem.

It was in part because of my own experience with anxiety-related problems that I decided, once my internship was over, to pursue the specialty of psychiatry. Specifically, I was interested in finding ways to help other young people who suffered from the same sorts of puzzling symptoms that had plagued me. After three years of psychiatric training, I began work in 1977 at Penn State's student health center. My timing could not have been better.

Not long after I started, a revolution began in our understanding of obsessive-compulsive disorder. First, researchers discovered a group of medications called the serotonin reuptake inhibitors (now including Prozac, Paxil, Zoloft, Luvox, Celexa, and Lexapro) that specifically treated OCD. Then came a remarkable new psychological treatment referred to as cognitive-behavioral therapy. Rather than exploring unconscious motivations, this treatment taught people to view their obsessions from more helpful perspectives, and to purposefully expose themselves to their worst fearful thoughts. When used alone, it was soon realized, either medications or cognitive-behavioral therapy could markedly help approximately two-thirds of OCD sufferers. Using the two treatments together sometimes resulted in an even better outcome.

By the late 1980s, most therapists specializing in obsessive-compulsive disorder had made cognitive-behavioral therapy their first-choice treatment. I found it worked marvelously well, far better than psychotherapies involving "empathetic listening" or attempts at uncovering emotional conflicts. And cognitive-behavioral therapy had this singular advantage over medications: once patients learned it, they could stop seeing a doctor and use it by themselves.

Around this time, I began to be intrigued when some of my patients with strong spiritual beliefs would report to me that their "faith" had helped them greatly in dealing with their obsessions. Despite the fact that I was by then a fully committed Christian, I never seriously considered that faith, or a certain aspect of it, might represent a specific therapy for obsessive-compulsive disorder. Religion and OCD, it seemed to me then, did not mix well. The reasons went beyond my own negative experience.

A number of my patients had suffered from religious fears that unmistakably aggravated their disorder. One devout Christian, for instance, had been driven to repeat her mealtime prayers over and over for half an hour or more, in a panic that she had offended God by not displaying a sufficient amount of devotion. A Jewish student had nervously guarded her Shabbat candles long into the night, hovering around them, compulsively mumbling prayers. Her obsession was that if they were accidentally blown out, God would cause her mother to die. All too often, I was forced to admit, it was a dreadful fear of God that was to blame for my patients' symptoms. I left religion alone, therefore, and used established treatments to help my patients.

Then, in the fall of 1995, I had an encounter with a student in a therapy group that caused me to reassess all my assumptions. Katey was a petite, smartly dressed girl, and also exceptionally insightful and articulate. At our first group session, she spoke up, shaky-voiced, and told us her story. "I can't stop really stupid thoughts from coming into my mind," she began. One difficult problem was the insistent idea that parasites were "all over" her hands. It drove her to wash again and again. "I go through so many paper towels it's unreal," she complained. Yet contamination fears were not the worst of her torments.

"I see knives sticking into things," Katey continued, sheepishly. While walking down the street, the shocking image of a dagger being plunged into a passerby would take over her mind. While petting her cat, she would see a bloody blade protruding from its neck. While praying, it would be a terrifying picture of God. She would imagine God as a hazy, rather indistinct old man—and, all of a sudden, there would be a knife sticking right into him.

Thoughts such as these caused Katey's heart to race and her stomach to tie in knots. To combat them she would attempt to rethink the images without the knives—to disarm them, as it were. But this proved frustratingly impossible, since, as Katey put it, "I know what I'm trying not to see, so it comes right back." Sometimes Katey would say a prayer to escape the anxiety and guilt she felt for having these thoughts. "God, forgive me for having them," she would repeat over and over. But the prayer didn't work, either. "I tell myself," Katey explained, "Stop all this crazy stuff! But at the same time I'm just too terrified to stop. Somehow, I think I'm responsible for these terrible thoughts, and I've got to do something to get rid of them."

Over the course of a college semester, Katey faithfully employed cognitive-behavioral therapy. She learned to view her obsessions and compulsions as a medical disorder. Systematically, in planned exercises, she exposed herself to the images that terrified her, and resisted performing compulsive counterimages and prayers. In one exercise, for instance, she focused her attention on a newspaper account of a bloody stabbing and told herself that she was to blame for it. Then she endured the terrifying anxiety that ensued until it faded away.

Katey made excellent progress. Her attacks of gut-wrenching anxiety fully remitted. Obsessional thoughts, although still a daily problem, no longer caused such agony—she was able to put up with them. It wasn't until our last group session, however, that she shared a remarkable observation. "My obsessions have really helped my spiritual condition," Katey said. "I give God the responsibility for them, and I've learned to trust God more than ever."

Fascinated, I asked her to tell us more. "I've discovered that what works best for my obsessions is to tell God that I'm leaving everything in his hands," she said. "If he wants my hands to be contaminated, that's okay. If he wants a knife to be sticking into someone, that's fine too. The whole thing is that my trust in God must be stronger than my obsessions. If it's not, then the obsessive-compulsive disorder wins."

Katey had said that she made God "responsible" for her obsessional thoughts. I was startled by her choice of that particular word. Her remarks resonated in an extraordinary manner with certain research findings that were being reported in major journals of psychiatry and psychology just at that time.

Several groups of investigators, led by Paul Salkovskis at Oxford University in England, were finding strong evidence that obsessive-compulsive disorder was uniquely connected to the assumption of responsibility, specifically to "feelings of excessive personal responsibility for harm that may occur to self and others." These researchers had demonstrated experimentally an intriguing fact: While obsessive-compulsive disorder sufferers are easily overwhelmed by the responsibility they imagine to rest on their own shoulders, they are also very good at giving responsibility to others.

Admittedly, this idea was not new. Many therapists had learned from experience that control of a particularly disruptive compulsion could be accomplished most quickly by a patient's giving to another person the responsibility for the fear that triggered the compulsion. For example, in the case of a homemaker who checked her stove's on-off control for hours at a time, the responsibility for preventing a fire from starting could be given to her spouse. Typically, however, this tactic would be employed only for a short time and only as a last resort. For one thing, there was concern that a patient would develop an unhealthy dependence on the person who was assuming responsibility. For another, this other person would probably tire, eventually, of this burden being placed on his shoulders.

Yet, as I remembered the recent research and related it to Katey's comments, I was struck anew by the therapeutic potential of transferring responsibility. What about a believer who gave responsibility to God? I wondered. Might that not be a healing type of dependence? And who better than God for taking burdens without tiring?

My curiosity was piqued, but I didn't know if this treatment really worked. There had been no research relevant to this approach. Furthermore, transferring responsibility to God, as opposed to a flesh-and-blood person, presented an array of potential difficulties. Were there examples beyond Katey's? I had read a good bit on Christians of centuries past. A few well-known individuals, I remembered, had likely suffered from obsessive-compulsive disorder. Maybe there was an answer in the historical record. Eagerly, I started on another search.

I knew that John Bunyan, author of the immensely influential seventeenth-century Puritan classic *The Pilgrim's Progress*, had been identified as a likely sufferer of what we would now call severe OCD. Indeed, his spiritual autobiography, *Grace Abounding to the Chief of Sinners*, was considered by many experts to be the most extraordinary personal account of the disorder ever written. I was also aware of three other historically important Christians whose apparently obsessive-compulsive symptoms had become a source of latter-day psychiatric speculation. They were Martin Luther, architect of Europe's sixteenth-century Reformation and a figure of incomparable importance in the history of Western civilization; Ignatius of Loyola, Luther's famous adversary, founder of the Catholic order known as the Jesuits and leader of the Counter-Reformation; and Alphonsus Liguori, a nineteenth-century Catholic saint who is renowned for his contributions to the field of moral theology.

Intrigued, I set myself to reading everything I could find on these three. Ignatius's autobiography, *A Pilgrim's Journey*, dictated near the end of his life in 1553, reveals that in his early thirties he suffered from severe anxieties that we would almost certainly call in the present day a mild case of OCD. Although Liguori left no autobiography, published notes from his journal together with accounts of his life written by fellow priests strongly suggest that he suffered from obsessions and compulsions of many different types that were longer lasting and more disabling than those of Ignatius.

Martin Luther's case took more digging. The American edition of Luther's complete works runs to fifty-five volumes, and sprinkled through them are references to many diverse experiences that might be interpreted in the present age as psychiatric symptoms. Biographers have agreed, by and large, that Luther suffered from some sort of a psychiatric condition during his life, but there has been no consensus as to its nature. In addressing the questions of whether Luther truly suffered from a bona fide psychiatric disorder, and if so, the nature of it, I was fortunate to benefit from the outstanding progress that has been made over the last few decades in precisely defining the core symptoms that characterize various psychiatric disorders. Utilizing this knowledge, a careful reading of pertinent works left me with little doubt that during Luther's early years in the monastery he was plagued by what we would now consider a textbook case of obsessive-compulsive disorder.

I next reviewed the lives of dozens of other religious notables who were known to have endured unusual trials and temptations. I found it fascinating to explore the letters of Jane de Chantal, a well-known Catholic saint of the sixteenth century who founded the Visitation Order of nuns. "My whole mind is just a confused turmoil, casting up feelings of rebellion, doubts and every other sort of horror," Jane wrote in one letter to a sister in her convent. "So vehement are these assaults, I feel as if I am ready to give up everything."[2] Jane attempted to deal with the horror in her mind by performing endless acts of adoration. Without a doubt, I soon concluded, Jane de Chantal was plagued by severe obsessions and compulsions.

I became especially enthralled by one saint in particular, Thérèse of Lisieux, the "Little Flower" of the Catholic church, a nineteenth-century French nun who enjoys extraordinary popularity among today's Catholics (not to be confused with Teresa of Avila from the sixteenth century). Before her early death at twenty-four, Thérèse achieved what some theologians have come to regard as a unique state of union with God. Her poetry, her prayers, and especially her moving spiritual autobiography, *Story of a Soul,* have touched the lives of millions. I was familiar with Thérèse's contributions, but I had never approached this winsome figure with the eye of a psychiatric detective. A thorough review of her autobiography, as well as of her many saved letters, however, convinced me that she, too, had suffered from obsessive-compulsive disorder.

All in all, I ended up with six seminal figures who evidently suffered from obsessive-compulsive disorder: John Bunyan, Ignatius of Loyola, Alphonsus Liguori, Martin Luther, Jane de Chantal, and Thérèse of Lisieux—an astounding list of Christian greats. Now the all-important question became how they dealt with their disorder. Did they find a cure? Was it the same as Katey's?

15

The six had varying degrees of success. Liguori and Jane de Chantal suffered from a lifelong affliction. While Liguori made considerable progress with his symptoms—thanks to sympathetic and insightful spiritual advisers—Jane made little progress with hers, and terrifying obsessions hounded her to her deathbed. Ignatius's case was different. Harassed with a relatively mild case of obsessive-compulsive disorder, he overcame it on his own after fully grasping the irrational nature of his obsessions. By sheer force of will he put a stop to his compulsive confessing.

Standing apart from these three cases were those of Luther, Bunyan, and Thérèse, which bore a striking likeness. All three, after enduring approximately a decade of severe obsessions and compulsions, experienced a similar, profound insight into the nature of God that worked as a specific antidote for their symptoms. They discovered that God would take responsibility for any and all of their tormenting fears if only they turned to him in trust. These three individuals subsequently made unconditional faith in the power and mercy of God the guiding light of their lives.

Modern theologians recognize an uncanny likeness among the mature religious beliefs of Luther, Bunyan, and Thérèse. Bunyan was a minister in a small Puritan sect to which the writings of Luther were virtually unknown. Yet, uniquely among English Puritan ministers, Bunyan came to adopt a religious philosophy that rested firmly, as noted by biographer Richard Greaves, on a "Lutheran foundation."[3] Thérèse, according to the noted twentieth-century Swiss theologian Hans Urs von Balthasar, represents nothing less than "the Catholic answer to the demands and questions raised by Luther."[4] Although the importance of faith is stressed throughout the Bible, especially in the letters of Paul, one wonders why Luther, Bunyan, and Thérèse would have all chosen to emphasize this one particular aspect of Christian belief to such an extent. They lived in different centuries and were members of widely divergent Christian denominations.

What explained the similarity? Surely, it seemed to me, it was the fact that all three had suffered from obsessive-compulsive disorder; and all had found, within the broad confines of their shared Christian faith, the same specific cure—the one that Katey had found. William James, the peerless American scholar of psychology and religion, demonstrated that an individual's religious beliefs are shaped by their psychological results. "If a creed makes a man feel happy, he almost invariabbly adopts it," James writes.[5] Perhaps Luther, Bunyan, and Thérèse all came to emphasize the same basic Christian truth because—from a purely psychological perspective—that was what worked for them. It represented, perhaps, the best treatment for obsessions and compulsions that they could have found.

1

Introduction

There are four main ideas in this book, the fruits of my search for evidence of a Christian cure for obsessions and compulsions. They speak to a complicated relationship between obsessive-compulsive disorder and Christianity, a reciprocal relationship of sorts. Christian teachings can, it appears, both trigger OCD and cure it. The disorder itself, on the other hand, through its effect on certain believers, has played a hidden role in the shaping of Christian doctrine.

The most important idea is this: that three of the greatest luminaries in the history of the Christian religion—Martin Luther, John Bunyan, and Saint Thérèse of Lisieux—all appear to have suffered from severe cases of what is now called obsessive-compulsive disorder, and all found the same way to overcome it through centering their lives on a single magnificent Christian truth.

The psychological struggles of Luther, Bunyan, and Thérèse form the core of this book, chapters 3, 4, and 5. Providentially, these three individuals were not only religious geniuses, but also literary geniuses. Their stories are gripping. I hope that

Christians who suffer from obsessive-compulsive disorder—my primary audience—will find it reassuring to read them. I hope these readers will recognize that their symptoms are nothing to be ashamed of when they discover that obsessions and compulsions appear to have affected some of God's favorite saints. Further, the reader who is tired from years of fighting obsessions and compulsions will find here the possibility of a cure based not on human effort, but rather on trust in God's merciful love. Chapter 8 presents a summary and analysis of this cure. Chapter 9, perhaps of most practical help to the Christian with active OCD symptoms, suggests a hands-on approach to applying it.

The book's second idea is that the cure arrived at by Luther, Bunyan, and Thérèse finds strong support in contemporary psychological research. Over the last three decades, psychologists have made immense strides in understanding obsessive-compulsive disorder. They have discovered certain attitudes and behaviors that make obsessional fears worse, and others that relieve them. Chapters 6, 7, and 8 summarize this modern understanding of OCD and its treatment and demonstrate that the cure of Luther, Bunyan, and Thérèse rests on therapeutic principles. It can even be viewed as a form of cognitive-behavioral therapy. These chapters may be especially useful to ministers, priests, and Christian counselors in the everyday conduct of therapy with OCD sufferers: offering direction in which Christian truths to emphasize, what to suggest that a patient pray for, and whether to encourage an individual to strongly reject an obviously sinful thought.

The third major idea, presented in chapter 2, is based on a broader historical observation. It seems clear from surviving evidence that an epidemic of clinical obsessive-compulsive disorder struck the West during that great flowering of individualism known as the Renaissance, and that it was in large part triggered by the emphasis placed on new Christian teachings that arose at that time. One of the lessons of this discovery is that Christians must always be cautious in how they apply the truths of their faith. Psychiatry has been slow to recognize any link between culture and mental disorder. The onslaught of obsessive-compulsive disorder that occurred during the Renaissance speaks to connections not yet fully explored between radical cultural change, new psychological stresses, the development of new religious practices, and the occurrence of particular mental disorders.

The fourth main idea of the book is treated in the epilogue. Theologians agree that the greatness of Luther, Bunyan, and Thérèse rests on the fact that through their writings and teachings, they brought Christianity back to a foundational truth of our faith that is often neglected: We can put absolute trust in the mercy of God, if only we turn to him in faith. In psychological terms, Luther, Bunyan, and Thérèse were driven to embrace this truth by their tormenting obsessions and compulsions. Can it not be argued, then, that OCD is more than just a disorder? Indeed, it can serve as a catalyst for great accomplishments.

Religion and Psychotherapy

The majority of psychiatrists and psychologists practicing in the present day object to the use of religious beliefs as a means of furthering psychotherapy.[1] To them, religion and psychotherapy simply don't mix. Since mixing the two is exactly what this book advocates, it is important to take a minute to examine this bias.

Essentially, it began with Sigmund Freud, the most famous psychiatrist of the twentieth century and the first great psychotherapist. Freud's goal was to develop a psychological treatment for mental disorders that was firmly rooted in scientific principles. To this end, he developed his famous treatment, psychoanalysis, in which the psychoanalyst's task is to help his patient put emergent psychological conflicts into a fully rational framework. To Freud, religious beliefs were merely fantasies, "wishful illusions."[2] His dim view of religion reflected the rationalism of Enlightenment thought, which held that the function of the mind was to process sensory information, and make sense of it in such a way as to allow the events of the world to be more predictable. In other words, the healthy mind was supposed to function something in the manner of a scientist, producing testable theories that were based on observation. Religious and spiritual beliefs could be of no use to such a mind, since they deal with the unseen rather than the seen, and are not empirically provable.

Psychoanalysis dominated psychiatry in America and parts of Europe for half a century. Not surprisingly, it usually had the direct effect of "curing" people from their religious beliefs. As the noted analyst Otto Fenichel explained in 1941, "Repeatedly I have seen that with the analysis of the sexual anxieties and with the maturing of the personality, the attachment to religion has ended."[3]

Though Freud's influence waned in the second half of the twentieth century, newer forms of therapy continued to incorporate the idea that psychological problems could be cured only if the sufferer came to a more scientific understanding of them. As recently as 1983, Albert Ellis, perhaps the most influential psychotherapist since Freud, could write that "devout belief and religiosity distinctly contribute to and in some ways are equal to mental or emotional disturbance [while] unbelief, skepticism, and thoroughgoing atheism not only abet but are practically synonymous with mental health."[4] All unscientific hypotheses, according to Ellis, are harmful when adopted as strong personal beliefs. At least through the 1980s, psychiatrists and psychologists, most of whom were nonreligious themselves, widely believed that religious and spiritual beliefs were a cause of mental illness, but never a cure. .

In the last decade of the twentieth century, a rapprochement of sorts finally began between psychiatry and religion. First, two widely reported national studies concluded that attendance at the spiritually based program Alcoholics Anonymous was the single most important factor in recovery from alcoholism.[5] Then, as researchers began to consider the role of religious belief more widely, more than a hundred studies reported rather convincing evidence that strong religious and spiritual beliefs are associated with a decreased incidence of a diverse group of problems ranging from depression and anxiety to violent outbursts and delinquency.[6]

The rationalist idea that the mind functions by gathering data to make the world predictable has also been questioned. In his 2001 book *Religion Explained*,Washington University's Pascal Boyer cites studies demonstrating that when presented with a choice between an explanation that makes an event more rationally understandable and an explanation that makes it less so, people just as frequently choose the latter.[7] The mind seems to have no natural bias toward finding rational explanations, he concludes, and furthermore a person is no happier or more well adjusted when it does so. What is important to the mind, according to evolutionary psychologists such as Boyer, is what works in a Darwinian sense, what works to help people survive. Religious ideas may be what works best.

Not surprisingly, there has been a surge of public interest in spiritual methods of therapy. National newspaper and magazine articles describe the healing properties of New Age philosophies, meditation techniques, and traditional Eastern and Western religious practices. A small but growing number of therapists now incorporate religious and spiritual practices into more conventional therapy. A 1999 poll, for instance, indicated that 15 percent of psychiatrists are willing to engage their patients in prayer.[8] Others incorporate the popular spiritual ideas advanced by New Age leaders such as Andrew Weil and Deepak Chopra.

One overarching problem, however, is that studies thus far have not pinpointed either how spiritual approaches work to foster mental health or under what circumstances they should be used. One can be left with the impression that prayer, scripture reading, Buddhist meditation, yoga, and a raft of other approaches are equally therapeutic for anything that ails anybody.

This book deals in particulars. It describes how one specific foundational Christian belief can be used to treat one widespread psychiatric problem of the present day—obsessive-compulsive disorder—through its application within guidelines of modern cognitive-behavioral therapy. It also demonstrates how certain exaggerations and misinterpretations of basic Christian ideas can make obsessive-compulsive disorder worse.

What about religious individuals who are not Christian—can they make use of these insights? I believe they can, although this book does not cover that territory. The great monotheistic religions, including Judaism and Islam, all share a view of an all-powerful God in whom one can put complete trust. It is nothing but this capacity for trust that Luther, Bunyan, and Thérèse used to cure their OCD.

Christian Therapy and OCD

At first glance, obsessive-compulsive disorder might seem to be the least likely of all mental disorders to benefit from any sort of religious psychotherapy or counseling. Since rituals of various types (e.g., repeated prayers) play a prominent role in both religion and OCD, many psychiatrists and psychologists have assumed that encouraging obsessionals to be more religious could be dangerous. It would be like encouraging an alcoholic to spend more time in bars.

Freud argued this point strongly. He believed in an essential equivalence between religious rituals and clinical compulsions. Going further, the great psychoanalyst actually contended that religion was itself a form of obsessive-

24

compulsive disorder. He proposed that just as obsessions and compulsions represented the neurotic remnants of an individual's childhood conflicts, religious beliefs and rituals were the pathological vestiges of society's growing pains. Thus, he could ultimately conclude that the religious convictions of billions of people constituted one great "universal obsessional neurosis."[9]

Subsequent researchers, however, have failed to find any direct connection. Studies published in the *Journal of the American Academy of Child and Adolescent Psychiatry* in the 1980s, for instance, demonstrated that superstitious and religious behaviors are observed no more often in young OCD sufferers than in the general population; and, further, that how often a child performs normal rituals, such as the use of lucky numbers or certain bedtime stories, has no relationship to the development of clinical obsessions and compulsions. Noted researcher Judith Rapoport of the National Institute of Mental Health, has concluded that the phenomena of clinical compulsions and religious rituals are "quite discontinuous."[10]

Although Freud was mistaken in suggesting an essential equivalence between religion and obsessive-compulsive disorder, he was correct in recognizing that religious teachings sometimes lead to the development of obsessions and compulsions. How does this happen? Cross-cultural studies reveal that the content of a person's obsessions depends on the society in which the person is raised. Reports from Israel, Saudi Arabia, and Bahrain reveal that in highly religious societies, obsessions most commonly involve religious concerns. In more secular cultures such as America and Western Europe, on the other hand, contamination obsessions are the type most commonly seen.

Experts now agree that clinical obsessions tend to deal with whatever ideas are potentially most fearful to an individual. Thus, obsessions of filth and contamination, so common among OCD sufferers in the present day, were relatively rare before the germ theory of disease became accepted in the 1800s. We can say that religion is a cause of obsessive-compulsive disorder, but only in the limited sense that it is often the substrate for the disorder.

Defining Clinical OCD

Obsessive-compulsive disorder is a specific psychiatric syndrome that is narrowly defined. It is important to be clear about its exact definition, because the research cited in this book, as well as the tentative conclusions drawn about the role of religion in its cause and treatment, do not necessarily apply to other similar disorders.

In one sense, diagnosing the disorder is simple. It requires the presence of only two symptoms. In practical terms:

> OCD is present when a person suffers from obsessions and compulsions, and they cause significant distress or disability.

The difficulty arises in recognizing these two symptoms. Unfortunately, the terms *obsession* and *compulsion* are somewhat confusing. They have come to be used popularly in such a loose manner that their original psychiatric meanings have been all but lost. The term *obsession,* for instance, is often employed for what is more accurately termed a preoccupation, such as a coach's "obsession" with winning. *Compulsion,* on the other hand, is used to indicate anything done to excess, like compulsively eating sweets. The two terms put together, "obsessive-compulsive," commonly describe an individual who is unusually perfectionistic, time-conscious, and nervously driven to succeed. None of these meanings, astonishingly, has much to do with clinical OCD.

The unique and distinct nature of clinical obsessions was recognized early on. In the nineteenth century, when psychiatry was first emerging as a medical specialty, the German psychiatrist Karl Westphal provided an excellent definition that has not since been surpassed. Here's a simple version:

> Obsessions are thoughts which come to the foreground of consciousness in spite of and contrary to the will of the patient, and which he is unable to suppress although he recognizes them as abnormal and not characteristic of himself.[11]

The current, authoritative *Diagnostic and Statistical Manual of American Psychiatry* (DSM-IV-R; see appendix A) provides a more lengthy but similar definition. Both Westphal and the manual stress four important qualities that set apart the ideas, images, and urges that are clinical obsessions from other kinds of thoughts.

Obsessions, first of all, are *intrusive* thoughts. They pop into the mind abruptly, interrupting the normal flow. They are also *recurrent*. They keep on coming back again and again, in exactly the same form. Obsessions are *unwanted*: they are gate-crashers, intruders in the night, and as a result, a person fights to get rid of them. Here, the clinical meaning of the term stays close to its Latin root, *obsidere*, meaning to besiege, as an army would attack a city for the purpose of forcing surrender. Lastly, obsessions are recognized as *inappropriate*. Given a chance to sit back and reflect for a minute, the individual just can't figure out why the tormenting thought would ever have occurred in the first place.

Clinical compulsions, the other half of the equation, are purely secondary phenomena, acts performed solely to put right a tormenting thought. An obsession strikes, anxiety mounts, and a repetitive act provides a temporary way out. For our purposes,

> Compulsions are repetitive acts that are clearly excessive, performed solely in order to lessen the anxiety caused by an obsession.

Compulsions may be either physical behaviors, such as checking or asking for reassurance, or purely mental acts, such as

27

conjuring up a pleasant image or repeating a phrase over and over in one's mind. Unfortunately, all compulsions share one basic quality: although they provide short-term respite from obsessions, in the long run they only make obsessions worse. Obsessions, in turn, make compulsions worse. It becomes a vicious cycle.

Sir Aubrey Lewis, considered by many the greatest English psychiatrist of the twentieth century, observed in 1935 that most cases of obsessive-compulsive disorder involve one of four fearful themes: filth, harm, lust, or blasphemy.[12] In Western cultures, where filth is the most common theme, obsessions typically involve the idea that one's hands have become contaminated. Often there are accompanying distressing images of germs or dirt. Usually, the response to such obsessions is compulsive washing. Not uncommonly, reassurance about possible contamination is endlessly requested from family members and medical professionals.

Almost as common is the theme of violent harm, which covers a wide range of obsessions and compulsions. One individual suffers the vivid image of being injured in an assault and must check her door again and again to assure safety. Another person is struck by the idea of his house catching fire, so he runs through his house, checking to make sure that the furnace, stove, light switches, and appliances are all turned off. Another has the fear while driving her car that she may have unknowingly struck someone. She repeatedly turns around and checks to make sure there has been no accident.

Tormenting lustful or sexual thoughts are less frequently seen. In my practice as a student health psychiatrist, these often involve homosexuality—not authentic homosexual desires, but rather sudden, completely unwanted images occurring in people who have no actual homosexual inclinations.

The religious theme, studies suggest, is relatively uncommon today in Western cultures, occurring in less than 10 percent of cases. In my practice, however, I see them more frequently, perhaps because I practice in a rural area where people tend to be very religious. Most commonly the patients I see suffer from either intrusive blasphemous statements, such as "f—— you, Jesus," or the more general idea that one is simply displeasing God. Frequent among Protestants is the obsessional fear of having committed the unforgivable sin of blasphemy against the Spirit (Matt. 12:31). Among Catholics, a time-honored and still common obsessive thought is that one has failed to confess all one's sins. The compulsions performed to ward off religious obsessions usually involve repeated prayers, Bible reading, and reassurance seeking. The middle chapters of this book will provide a plenitude of examples.

When I was in training, the overall incidence of obsessive-compulsive disorder was thought to be extremely low. The figure most commonly quoted was a minuscule one-twentieth of one percent of the adult population. What was not appreciated, however, was how adept OCD sufferers are at keeping their disorder hidden. In 1983, when the National Institutes of Health announced the findings of the first large-scale study on the incidence of mental health disorders in the U.S. population, the results took mental health professionals completely by surprise: OCD was found to occur in 1.9 to 3.3 percent of the population.[13] The experts had been off by more than 4,000 percent in their estimate of the incidence of this disorder.

Yet even that oft-quoted figure is probably too low. The criteria used for the diagnosis of obsessive-compulsive disorder in the 1983 survey, called the Diagnostic Interview Schedule, were very strict. Individuals were said to suffer from OCD only if they had taken medication or sought a physician's help. More recent surveys that include all individuals who suffer significant distress as a result of obsessions and compulsions suggest a considerably higher incidence. A study from Zurich, Switzerland, for instance, concluded that 5.5 percent of people have suffered from such symptoms by age thirty. A reasonable estimate is that 5 to 10 percent of people suffer from at least a mild case of obsessive-compulsive disorder at some time during their lives.

It is not generally appreciated that the overall incidence of specific psychiatric disorders varies throughout history. Cases of hysteria, such as the sudden onset of blindness for purely psychological reasons, were rather common in the 1800s and a favorite topic in the writings of Freud. We see them rarely now. Obsessive-compulsive disorder became an epidemic in the Renaissance, as will be explained in the next chapter. Here the reader will find that, at first glance, Freud's gloomy assessment of the relationship of Christianity and OCD appears to be borne out.

Renaissance Anxieties

The term *Renaissance* is used in a broad sense to describe the era in Western Europe between the years of 1300 and 1600, when medieval civilization gave way to modern ways of thinking. Literally, it means "new birth." As noted by historian Basil Oldham, "The Renaissance marks a break in the world's history such as cannot elsewhere be equaled."[1] Among the new developments were unparalleled scientific and geographical discoveries, and revolutionary trends in literature, architecture, and the fine arts.

The greatest change of all, many believe, took place at a psychological level: in a person's sense of self. The distinguished Renaissance expert Jacob Burckhardt wrote in 1860 that the central development of the era was "the emergence of individualism."[2] Modern historians continue to echo this idea. Agnes Heller, writing in 1967, observes that the hallmark of the Renaissance was "an ever more individualistic outlook, sense of values, and way of behaving."[3] As a *New York Times Magazine* celebration of the "Me Millennium" phrased it:

A thousand years ago, when the earth was reassuringly flat and the universe revolved around it, the ordinary person had no last name, let alone any claim to individualism. The self was subordinated to church and king. Then came the Renaissance explosion of scientific discovery and humanist insight and, as both cause and effect, the rise of individual self-consciousness. All at once, it seemed, Man had replaced God at the center of earthly life.[4]

In the Middle Ages, people had felt incapable of influencing most of what mattered in their lives. The air was infested with spirits directing events. The stars and clouds were guided by angels. Lifelong roles were foreordained in heaven, assigned in childhood, and lived out in earth's stagnant feudal system in a sort of timeless blur. It was only with the rise of individualism that the average person—or, at least the average adult male—began to believe that he could determine his own destiny. As never before, new vistas opened for the individual.

There was also, however, a significant downside to this sense of empowerment. The new focus on the self introduced a new dimension of concern. The feeling of increased ability meant magnified responsibility. More opportunities to succeed meant more chances to flounder. The door was opened to a new plague of worries centered on the uncertainties of self-determination.

Renaissance Christians, it appears, seldom questioned the major tenets of their faith. For many, the concern that over-shadowed all others was whether one would reside eventually in heaven or in hell. Yet the church in this revolutionary era sometimes proved a source of anxiety more than of consolation. The reason can be traced to the fact that official Christianity—that is, the Roman Catholic church—actively promoted the Renaissance ideal of self-determination and empowerment of the individual.

It has been argued, in fact, that the driving force behind the Renaissance was the church's scholastic movement, which put a new emphasis on the importance of mankind's use of reason. Before that movement, people did not have to think much about their relationship with God; all church members in good standing could feel secure that they would live eternally in heaven after death. In scholasticism's wake, however, each Christian was expected to closely examine where he or she stood. The responsibility for attaining eternal life was placed to a greater degree than ever before on the shoulders of the individual. As historian Thomas Tentler observed in his 1977 book, *Sin and Confession on the Eve of the Reformation,*

> The fundamental assumption became that the average Christian can know and weigh his sins, because the church teaches [that] rational man is free and responsible, and he can apply this teaching to his life.[5]

Early in the Renaissance, a new intellectual discipline arose in the Catholic church, its task was to clarify the nature and gravity of the sins for which a person should be held responsible. Moral theology came to assume a central role in the teachings of Catholicism, and as time passed, moral theologians put ever greater burdens on the faithful. While prior to the Renaissance there were only three sins that would inevitably cause a person to lose salvation (murder, adultery, and idolatry), by its end there were literally hundreds. In the area of sexual behavior alone, thirteen different types of sinful acts were defined and categorized, and the seriousness of each was further broken down according to the degree of genuine contrition that was felt by the sinner.

The assumption of personal responsibility for this whole range of new concerns ushered in the era of the guilty conscience. "The concentration on the individual [led to] a preoccupation with sin," notes historian John Mahoney. "As moral theology concerned itself increasingly with the darker side of human existence, it increased men's moral apprehension and sense of guilt."[6]

33

Modern Catholic writers fully recognize the church's excesses during this period. As noted by leading moral theologian Ladislas Orsy of Georgetown University, author of *The Evolving Church and the Sacrament of Penance*,

> With the Renaissance came an inflation of mortal sins to an excess that today we recognize as absurd . . . the Christian conscience was invaded by an exaggerated theology of sin . . . hell became a greater menace for the Christian community than it ever was in the gospel. Damnation became a close threat hanging over the people.[7]

Epidemics of Psychopathies

Especially in the later stages of the era, the overburdened conscience of the Renaissance caused an onslaught of psychiatric illnesses. Psychiatrist Gregory Zilboorg in his widely cited textbook *History of Medical Psychology*, observes that "the number of the mentally ill reached alarming proportions" causing entire "epidemics of psychopathies."[8]

One epidemic took the form of what we now label as anorexia nervosa, a psychiatric disorder manifested in a refusal to eat. In his popular 1985 book, *Holy Anorexia*, Rudolph Bell points out that self-starvation was commonplace among nuns in the Renaissance, and concludes that approximately half fasted to the detriment of their health.[9] In some cases, at least, starvation appears to have been brought on primarily by overwhelming religious anxiety and guilt.

Major depression also appears to have become unusually widespread in the late Renaissance. This disorder is diagnosed when a person shows a severely depressed mood, a loss of interest and motivation, and withdraws from usual activities. In *Elizabethan Malady*, Lawrence Babb analyzes references to melancholy in diverse literary works, finding that while they are almost nonexistent in the early Renaissance, by the 1600s they are a principal theme in prose, drama, and biography. Babb concludes that the late Renaissance was characterized by "an epidemic of melancholy." The poet John Donne, who offered sonnets to the "Holy Sadness of the Soul," provided a vivid description of this malady, which he himself knew well: "God has seen fit to give us the dregs of misery, an extraordinary sadness, a predominant melancholy, a faintness of heart, a cheerlessness, a joylessness of spirit."[10]

Two other epidemics of psychopathology sprang up in the Renaissance that shared close similarities. Both were characterized by tormenting anxiety. Both involved intrusive, tormenting thoughts that a person could not dismiss from the mind. Both involved senseless and repetitive acts performed to allay the anxiety that was caused by the tormenting thoughts. These two epidemics were viewed as separate problems by Renaissance observers, probably because they were presumed to have differing causes: one being traceable to the weakness of the individual, and the other to attacks from Satan. Present-day psychiatrists, however, have no difficulty recognizing the more severe forms of both as manifestations of one illness: obsessive-compulsive disorder.

Obsessing about Minor Sins: Scrupulosity

The word *scruple* is derived from the Latin *scrupulum*, meaning a tiny pebble. In the present day, "scrupulous" often connotes outstanding moral integrity. In past centuries, however, the meaning was different. In the Renaissance, a moral connotation took hold: a scruple was a minute concern that needlessly upset a delicate conscience. *Scrupulous* described certain people who were tortured by nagging feelings that they might have committed a sinful act. In more difficult cases, these individuals would be driven to compulsively seek reassurance from others that they had not actually sinned.

35

Historians of the Catholic church suggest that severe cases of scruples were relatively rare before the thirteenth century.[11] By the end of the Renaissance, however, scrupulosity had become a virtual epidemic: mild cases were considered normal, and large numbers of guilt-ridden Christians suffered desperately. The advent of scrupulosity mirrored new developments in the Catholic rite of confession.

In this important sacrament, a believer confides his sins to a priest who, acting on behalf of God, absolves the sinner of responsibility. The priest typically prescribes a penance, an act of self-sacrifice such as a fast, that the individual must perform to atone for sins committed. Confession had always played a role in Christianity, providing a means of restoring individuals who had committed serious sins back into the body of the faithful. In the early centuries, however, confession was made openly, in public, and reserved for sins that seriously damaged the fabric of the community. In the seventh century, Irish monks introduced the practice of private confession and encouraged the revealing of lesser sins. Still, there was no formal obligation to confess, and most laypeople didn't, at least until their deathbed. This situation changed dramatically in the year 1215.

It was then, at the church's famous Fourth Lateran Council, that Pope Innocent III proclaimed that all Christians should confess their sins to a priest on a regular basis. In short order, confession was elevated from a legal matter between the individual and the church to a sacrament, or sacred rite. By the end of the thirteenth century, confession of sins was considered divinely instituted, obligatory, and necessary for the remission of sins.

The idea of regular confession was in line with the new ideals that stressed empowerment of the individual. The pope, reasonably enough, wanted to ensure that each person could avail himself or herself of the opportunity to receive forgiveness of sins. In the early centuries of regular confession, however, the result proved disastrous for many. The reason for this was the way that confession was carried out.

Too often it turned into an outright interrogation—a search for sin even where none was apparent. The confessor, who was likened to a physician, needed to minutely explore the extent of disease in a person's soul. He was to conduct a detailed inquiry into the nooks and shadows of an individual's conscience. Surviving "penitential manuals," handbooks instructing priests on how to carry out confession, provide a detailed description of the process. Usually, an inquiry into the presence of one of the seven deadly sins was the starting point.

One manual entitled "On the Confession of Masturbation" illustrates the audacious style of confession that was encouraged by some writers. When addressing a young, healthy man, the priest was to ask a series of specific questions about sexuality, such as: "Friend, do you remember when you were young, about ten or twelve years old, that your penis ever stood erect? Did you touch or rub your penis? For how long?"[12]

The goal of such confessions was to provoke an acute sense of fear over the possible loss of salvation. Indeed, William of Auvergne, author of a well-known thirteenth-century guide, wrote that in the conduct of confession there was "nothing to fear but the lack of fear."[13] As confession took shape primarily as an inquisition, many confessions, as noted by Tentler, "led to psychological and spiritual disaster."[14] People of tender conscience were driven to agonizing states of anxiety over minor sins that they may have committed.

An example of an individual who suffered briefly from severe scruples was Ignatius of Loyola (1495–1556), the towering Catholic saint who led the Counter-Reformation and founded the teaching order known as the Jesuits. Ignatius's scruples began in his early thirties, immediately after he had abandoned a promising magisterial career, given up all his earthly possessions, and become a wandering monk. In his autobiography the saint describes the malady that overtook him.

Although I made confession, there still remained some things which I thought I had not confessed. After confessing, my scruples returned, each time becoming more minute, so that I became quite upset. Although I knew that these scruples were doing me much harm and that it would be good to be rid of them, I could not shake them off.[15]

Ignatius makes clear the misery, and even suicidal tendencies, that can result from a such a case. "No trial would have been too great for me to bear, if I thought there was any hope of finding help," he writes, adding, "While these thoughts were tormenting me, I was frequently seized with the temptation to throw myself into a pit."[16]

It is worth noting how Ignatius carefully analyzed his fearful thoughts. He divided scruples into two groups. "Common scruples" involved incorrect assumptions about church teachings that could be easily corrected. Ignatius provides this example: "I accidentally step on a cross made by straws, and form the erroneous judgment that I have sinned." A second and more serious form of scruples was different. In these cases, the scruple had an alien quality. "The thought that I have sinned comes from without," Ignatius writes. Furthermore, these more serious scruples were disturbingly repetitive, and frustratingly difficult to shake off. "I have the thought that I have sinned, while on the other hand, there is the thought that I have not sinned. In all this I feel disturbed."[17]

In this insightful analysis Ignatius defined, perhaps for the first time in history, the core elements of what is called today a clinical obsession and differentiated an obsession from what we would call a common worry.

Horrible Thoughts of Blasphemy

The second epidemic of obsessional thoughts that occurred during the Renaissance took the form of blasphemous ideas, urges, and images. While scruples entailed exaggerated fear over having committed a sin that others would recognize as minor, these blasphemous thoughts seemed so vile that no one would deny their wickedness. As with scruples, there were mild cases that caused little disruption of people's lives. Other cases, however, caused agonizing torment and provoked severe compulsions such as endlessly repeated prayers and acts of faith.

Occasional reports of monks who suffered from "abominable thoughts and words against God" date back to the early centuries of the church. In the seventh century Saint John Climacus described a monk who was cruelly tormented for twenty years by "horrible thoughts of blasphemy," which he rejected through the use of contrary acts such as "fasts, watchings, and great austerities."[18] Such cases, however, were rare and seemingly confined to members of religious orders. In the Renaissance, the problem of horrible thoughts became a common malady.

Again, the shift appears traceable to changes in Catholic doctrine. In this case, the trigger appears to have been the judgment of moral theologians that entertaining a thought can be just as sinful as performing an act. Having the idea to stab another person, for example, could be as grave a sin as actually committing the crime. Moral theologians justified this conclusion by quoting from the Bible. On one occasion, for instance, Jesus stressed the harsh verdict that would fall on those who entertained thoughts of murder (Matt. 5:21). This interpretation, however, represented a radical departure from what had previously been taught. In earlier times only acts, and not thoughts, were matters for official church inquiry and discipline. When the church made the thinking of certain thoughts a mortal sin, it opened the door to a plague of obsessional fears.

Theologians wrote volumes on the criteria for distinguishing which thoughts were potentially sinful, as well as on the specific conditions under which the thinking of them actually constituted a sin. Basically, any thought against God or another person was a

39

cause for serious concern. The threshold of culpability, in theory, came to be whether a person consented to the thought's presence. A passing idea, in other words, was not necessarily a cause for alarm; but if an individual let certain thoughts remain in his or her mind, then he or she was guilty of a serious transgression. Renaissance Christians, therefore, were instructed to do everything in their power to immediately dismiss from their minds any thoughts of a potentially sinful nature. Thomas à Kempis's *Imitation of Christ*, next to the Bible the most popular Christian book of the Renaissance, reflects this counsel.

> The enemy suggests many evil thoughts. . . . Say to him, "Away, unclean spirit! Shame miserable creature! You are but filth to bring such things to my ears! . . . I would rather die and suffer all torture than consent to you! Be still! Be silent!"[19]

If one assumes the Christian perspective of the age, this advice seems perfectly reasonable for most situations, such as when an individual has a genuine urge to hurt someone. In other instances, however, such advice can be catastrophic. Suppose a young mother becomes aware of a passing idea to stab her beloved child. It is now known that such strange and repugnant ideas are commonplace. Most people readily dismiss them as mental rubbish. To a Renaissance Christian of tender conscience, however, such a thought assumes an extreme significance. In view of the teachings of her church, she must fight the thought with all her might or risk losing eternal life. Unfortunately, the very fighting of the thought only makes it come back stronger. The result is that the thought becomes a clinical obsession, and the ensuing battle in the mind produces gut-wrenching agony.

An outstanding example of an individual affected by severe obsessional thoughts of this nature is that of the famous Renaissance nun Saint Jane de Chantal. Widowed and wealthy at twenty-nine, she fought off suitors and finally renounced her worldly position to become a full-time religious. A woman of great intelligence and astonishing energy, over the course of her long life she founded her own religious order, the nuns known as The Visitation, and established more than eighty chapter-houses. Even as she was accomplishing many great deeds, however, she was hounded by obsessions. Jane writes,

> My mind is sometimes, often indeed, a bewildering confusion of darkness, powerlessness, thoughts, rebellions, doubts, disapproavals, and endless miseries. When the evil is at its height no respite comes to me, and so inexpressible is the pain that I know not what I would not do to rid myself of it. . . . The torment is inexplicable, yet it does not interfere with my application to other things, nor hinder me from writing or transacting business.[20]

Jane attempted to rid her mind of her torment by occupying herself with holy meditations. "I compel myself to make acts of union and of adoration," she writes. Some of her holy acts undoubtedly represented what would now be termed clinical compulsions.

Her mental agonies never relented. "I don't know what I would not do and suffer to be rid of this torture," she writes at age sixty-five. Finally, Jane asked to be relieved as mother superior of her convent. "My soul is in such a miserable and wretched condition," she explained to her sisters. "Should not I be in the hands of a good mother who will guide me in this state of moral abjection and of most painful blindness?" Her request to step down was rejected. Everyone agreed that, in spite of her tormenting anxieties, she was a marvelous mother superior.

How the Church Dealt with Scruples and Blasphemous Thoughts

In the case of scruples, priests quickly identified the epidemic on their hands: to their dismay, it was manifest openly in their

41

confessionals. The most esteemed French priest of the 1300s, Jean Gerson, to whom *Imitation of Christ* is sometimes attributed, described the problems created by the scrupulous, both for the individual confessing and for the priest confessor:

> It is impossible for them to be sufficiently contrite for their sins. They always have a scruple that they have not yet properly confessed. They exhaust themselves and their confessors with repeated confessions, especially of light and unimportant sins.[21]

Sometimes, the scrupulous were treated with no compassion at all. According to the official teachings of the church, scrupulous confessing could be considered a spiritual vice, because it indicated a lack of confidence in both God and the priest hearing confession. Saint Antoninus of Florence advised confessors, "As to those who want to confess too often, assign a certain time to hear them; do not make yourself available to them for other conversations; and always use not soft but harsh and severe words with them."[22] It is not difficult to imagine the effect of such words on sensitive, overanxious Renaissance Christians.

Fortunately, it appears that most often priests did treat the scrupulous gently, recognizing that they were in the grips of a sickness rather than a vice. Gerson emphasized a compassionate approach. In confession, he suggested, the priest should attempt to remove the excessive guilt that people feel for their minor sins by reminding them that "God does not demand anything beyond man's power."[23] The fourteenth-century Dominican theologian Johannes von Dambach wrote with great wisdom that in the case of the scrupulous, the priest should always provide "simple mercy" and encourage the penitent to "hope trustingly in the Lord."[24]

Some priests, courageously, openly criticized the church for its extreme hairsplitting on the nature of sin. Von Dambach, for instance, complained, "If a scrupulous man were to confess all those things that have been written for confessions, he well might need to keep a confessor in his purse!"[25] As time passed, compassionate treatment of the scrupulous became the rule.

The treatment of those people who suffered from blasphemous thoughts was different. Often it depended largely on whether the affected individual was a full-time religious (a priest or nun) or a lay parishioner. In the religious life, a person was expected to face severe spiritual trials. Saint Thomas Aquinas, the great thirteenth-century thinker who set the theological course of the Renaissance, declared that to become a priest or nun represented "a second baptism, a restoration of the sinner to a complete state of innocence."[26] In order to achieve this new start, however, the individual had to undergo a furious battle with the powers of hell. It was generally acknowledged that those who were most dear to God were most tested. In the case of priests and nuns, therefore, horrible blasphemous thoughts were an expected attack by the devil. Monastics who suffered from blasphemous thoughts were most often treated with compassion.

The unfortunate laypeople who suffered from such thoughts, however, were usually not treated so sympathetically. Sometimes they were even accused of being witches. It is clear from both civil and church records that the presence of horrible thoughts was often taken as a sign of demonic possession. In a case recorded in Kent, England, in 1584, justice of the peace Reginald Scott writes of a woman brought before him on charges of witchery. Mrs. Davie, "a good wife," admitted to having evil thoughts to harm her family. The prosecutors wanted her executed. Scott ruled, however, that "she hurt no one except, by her imagination, herself. . . . No one in his right wits would believe her."[27] Many who suffered from horrible thoughts, however, were not so fortunate in those who judged them.

It was the latter part of the Renaissance that witnessed the height of Christian intolerance and bigotry. The Inquisition held absolute power, witch-hunting was commonplace, and people accused of being satanic were often burned at the stake. In *Mystical Bedlam,* Michael MacDonald points out that "few of the people who thought they were possessed by the devil suffered from insanity or displayed spectacular symptoms. Most of them complained of anxiety, religious fears, and evil thoughts."[28] There is no telling how many individuals with what we now recognize as OCD suffered terrible fates.

It is possible that these twin epidemics—of scruples and of horrible thoughts—represented history's first widespread occurrence of obsessive-compulsive disorder. These epidemics also had a telling effect on the lives and contributions of a small group of highly influential individuals—people who changed the shape of Christian belief, even the course of history, in finding a specific Christian cure for their disorder.

Martin Luther

A Monk Crucified by His Thoughts

Martin Luther belongs to that select group of individuals who can be said to have changed the course of history. "No person save Columbus has left such a deep impression on our modern age," wrote Ralph Waldo Emerson.[1] Another noted historian observes, "It is safe to say that every person in Western Europe and in America is another person altogether from what he or she would have been had Martin Luther not lived."[2]

Luther's influence derives from the fact that he single-handedly launched the sixteenth-century Protestant Reformation, a revolt against the powerful and often corrupt Catholic church of his time, which propelled Europe into a century of tumultuous social and political upheaval. Some historians have viewed the Reformation as a bane for mankind. The religious wars it caused were some of the bloodiest in history and were not confined to Protestants fighting Catholics. Luther's intolerance of dissenters within his own fold contributed to wide-scale atrocities against minority Protestant sects. Most commonly, however, historians have emphasized the positive, seeing the Reformation as an epoch-making event that shaped the Enlightenment and brought a new sense of intellectual freedom throughout Europe.

For Luther himself, only one thing mattered a great deal: his religious teaching. He believed that God had called him to expose the heresy of the Catholic church, and to convert people to the true Christian faith. Almost a billion Protestants in the present day owe their religious identity to Luther's insights. Over the centuries, Luther's theological legacy has extended to more than a billion Catholics, as well. The sweeping reforms of the sixteenth-century Council of Trent adopted many of Luther's insights. In 1998, the Holy See went so far as to officially acknowledge the essential truth of Luther's most basic theological premise, "justification by faith alone."

That Luther has swayed the lives of so many is due, in part, to an extraordinary collection of personal traits. He was charismatic, bullheaded, and fearless, while at the same time a superb analytic thinker and highly talented as a writer and speaker. Luther also possessed an astounding capacity for work and mercilessly drove himself to a series of accomplishments equalled by few men.

Luther's great influence is also the result of a quirk in the politics of his time. Only his chance relationship with a powerful German prince kept him from certain execution as a heretic. There was another factor that played a part in Luther's fame: he was driven to his theological insights by a desperate need to find a cure for his own agonizing psychological problems.

Controversy about Luther's Mental State

The mental state of Martin Luther has perhaps generated more arguments than that of any other individual in history. Some people have insisted that Luther was insane, or psychotic. Others have maintained that he was completely normal. Among those who have taken a middle course, suggesting that he suffered some sort of moderate psychiatric condition, there has been endless debate as to what that condition could have been.

From the moment Luther first publicly challenged the teachings of his own Catholic church at a famous debate held in Worms, Germany, in 1521, Catholic apologists began a vigorous campaign to prove that he was unstable and demon-possessed. Luther's most implacable foe was a priest and scholar who met Luther at that debate, Johannes Cochlaeus. Three years before Luther's death, he wrote a highly influential biography of Luther that contained many unsubstantiated rumors.[3] One was a "fit in choir" during Luther's early monastery years. While chanting a Bible passage about a demon spirit (Mark 9:17), the story goes, Luther collapsed to the floor and screamed, "It's not me. It's not me!" This, according to Cochlaeus, was proof that Luther was possessed. This theory was widely accepted and promulgated by Catholics of the era. The venerable Pietro Vergerio, papal nuncio to Germany, assured the faithful, "On the basis of what I have found out about his birth, I am quite inclined to assume that Luther is possessed by a demon."[4]

The Enlightenment of the 1700s cast doubt on demonic theories, leading Catholic polemists to shift their emphasis to proving that Luther was insane from natural causes. The historian Ignaz von Döllinger wrote that Luther was "so overwhelmed by such a gloomy, depressing state of mind that he developed wildly confused, contradictory and destructive ideas that dominated his whole life and thought."[5] Well into the first half of the twentieth century, Catholic biographers continued to tarnish Luther with the brush of mental illness. In 1911 respected Jesuit scholar Hartmann Grisar wrote that Luther was a pathological "megalomaniac," his mental imbalance so severe that it prevented rational thinking.[6]

Protestant biographers, not surprisingly, attributed quite different psychological health to Luther. They countered, equally stridently, that Luther had never suffered any mental disorder at all. Luther, they believed, was a prophet, an individual chosen by God to reveal the truth. Like the prophets in the Old Testament, God had tested him with unusual trials, and Luther's responses to these trials were entirely reasonable. This view was first advanced by Luther's colleagues John Matthesius and Philipp Melanchthon, and it continued to be the official line of all Protestant writers into the early twentieth century.

For more than four hundred years, then, Catholics accused Luther of being so unstable that he couldn't think straight, while Protestants denied that he had ever suffered any significant psychological problems at all. These two mistaken attitudes—dismissal of an individual's accomplishments and denial of the illness—remain common biases in the present day toward people who suffer from psychiatric disorders. In the case of Luther, however, a clear-headed consensus on the general state of his mental health did finally develop over the last fifty years.

By the 1950s, Luther scholarship had advanced to the point where an authoritative collection of his correspondence and theological writings was published, in a massive eighty-six-volume Weimar edition. Historians could finally agree about which of the reported incidents in Luther's life could be taken as fact. Biographers even reached basic agreement on Luther's mental state: yes, in his early years he suffered from some sort of severe psychological problems; no, he was never insane, incapacitated, or lacking in extraordinary analytic ability. This consensus should have set the stage for psychiatrists to identify the nature of Luther's problems. Unfortunately, it did not.

Two twentieth-century psychiatrists wrote major works on Luther, but they only caused confusion. In 1937 Danish psychiatrist Paul Reiter published a two-volume analysis entitled *Martin Luthers Umwelt, Charakter und Psychose*. Reiter concludes that throughout Luther's life his "psychic balance was not complete." Luther's astounding achievements were the result of

48

"episodes of manic productivity."[7] Reiter diagnoses Luther as suffering from a severe and degenerative psychiatric condition that began in his early twenties and subsequently developed into a frank psychosis, a loss of contact with reality. For Reiter, Luther's conversations with Satan represent strong proof that he became psychotic. Reiter's analysis, however, was short on evidence, and psychiatrists and historians alike criticized it from the start.

In 1958 celebrated psychoanalyst Erik Erikson wrote *Young Man Luther*, a much more careful and thoughtful analysis than Reiter's. His biography went on to win the Pulitzer Prize. He describes Luther's tormenting anxieties with great care, drawing a bead on his "confused conscience." He identifies both Luther's "obsessive scrupulosity" and "compulsive" confessing. Unfortunately, for the sake of lasting clarity on Luther's diagnosis, Erikson concludes that obsessive-compulsive disorder represented only a minor part of a larger psychiatric problem: a "borderline psychotic state secondary to reawakened infantile conflicts."[8]

Erikson postulates that Luther's father treated him in an unusually harsh and sadistic manner, causing repressed conflicts. A critical problem with his analysis, however, is that there is no good evidence that Luther suffered any unusual difficulties in childhood; and on the contrary, some evidence suggests that Luther was especially close to his father. In a rejoinder to Erikson's work, entitled *Psychohistory and Religion*, historian Roger Johnson goes so far as to label Erikson's work "a very shoddy piece of speculation."[9] The majority of Luther experts strongly reject Erikson's analysis.

With no credible help from psychiatrists, Luther's twentieth-century biographers have also reached widely divergent conclusions regarding the nature of his psychological problems.[10] Roland Bainton in his engaging 1952 biography *Here I Stand*, the most widely published study of Luther in English, made perhaps the wisest assessment. He notes that Luther as a young man was "on the verge of a nervous collapse," but as to the precise nature of the disorder, Bainton discreetly concludes, "The question can be better faced when more data becomes available."[11]

The data are available now. In the last twenty years, advances in the understanding of mental illnesses have ascertained that diagnosing a psychiatric disorder does not require speculating on childhood conflicts. What it does require is a careful analysis of a patient's symptoms. In deciding which, if any, psychiatric diagnosis applies to Martin Luther's problems, what is crucial is to look carefully at the facts of his life, and particularly at what he himself says about the torments that he suffered.

Luther's Beginnings

Martin Luther was born in 1483 in Eisleben, a small village in rural north-central Germany equidistant between Hamburg two hundred miles to the west and Berlin to the east. It is a beautiful area of Germany, known for its rolling hills and vast green forests. Except for a few trips, Luther spent his entire life in the towns located near his birthplace.

Luther's father, Hans, was a copper miner. He was a rugged and ambitious man who, by the time of Martin's birth, had risen from poverty to become the manager of several mines. Hans was a strict disciplinarian at home, as were most fathers, and he whipped young Martin for the slightest error. Despite such treatment, Martin was always extremely devoted to his father, and named a son after him.

Part of the reason for Hans's success in the mines was his marriage to Margaret Lindemann, a woman from a prosperous family that guaranteed his business loans. Margaret, like Hans, was strong-willed and hardworking. A passionate believer in the Catholic faith, she taught her four sons that what was most important in this life was preparing for the next. Margaret, like many people of that time, was also very superstitious. She believed, for instance, that witches from the forest turned themselves into mice and stole the family's food. Young Martin did not doubt these stories, and throughout his life he remained convinced of the power of witchcraft and magic.

Martin's parents recognized him as unusually bright, and sacrificed to send him to special schools. There, he proved to be an able student. He also became a fine musician, proficient on the lute and a good singer. He was physically strong and energetic. As far as can be told, throughout his school years Martin Luther was well liked by his peers, knew how to have fun, and caused no problems for anyone. Hans and Margaret saw the prospects of his making an excellent marriage and then supporting them in their old age. They encouraged him to become a lawyer, and Martin, a dutiful son, embarked on the study of law at the University of Erfurt at age twenty.

From a psychological point of view, the only thing that may have set young Martin apart from his peers while growing up was an unusual sensitivity—a guilt-proneness and a sense of unease about his eternal salvation. Luther once said that when growing up he had always "horribly feared the last day." At age fourteen, his attention was riveted by the sight of an emaciated monk he saw on the street, who, it turned out, was a prince who had sacrificed his fortune to live a life of poverty. Comparing the monk to himself, Martin was gripped by overwhelming shame. As he approached his twenties, his uneasiness increased. In his last year in college, moodiness plagued him.[12]

Six months into law school an event occurred that would change Luther's life forever. He was journeying back to school on foot, after a visit home to his parents. About four miles from Erfurt, he encountered a thunderstorm, and was thrown to the ground by the force of lightning striking nearby. Terror-stricken, perhaps having what would now be called a panic attack, he prayed that he would not die and promised that if he lived, he

51

would become a monk. Whether Luther had been seriously considering the religious life prior to the thunderstorm is unknown. He would later explain only this to his angered father: "Suddenly surrounded by the terror and the agony of death, I felt constrained to make my vow."[13]

Two weeks after the thunderstorm Martin Luther walked through the doors of an imposing monastery in Erfurt and was accepted as a novice in the Augustinian order of monks.

The Early Monastery Years

The Augustinians were known for their discipline and austerity. They sought to assure their place in heaven through a combination of devotion and self-sacrifice. Life in the monastery was isolated, demanding, and somber. Novices were assigned small, bare, unheated rooms for sleep, study, and prayer. Small windows in their doors allowed them to be observed at all times. Talking was forbidden except with one's superior. Seven times a day, starting at 2 a.m., the monks gathered together in choir for their main activity, chanting the Psalms.

Luther did not take to this life. During his second year in the monastery, severe problems began to surface. He could not escape the worry that he was unfit to be "saved." Instead of going to heaven at the end of his time on earth, he would be consigned to hell. For approximately a decade, Luther suffered tormenting symptoms of anxiety that injured his health and destroyed his self-confidence. At times, he was close to a complete breakdown.

In his later years, Luther did not shy away from describing the mental agonies that he had endured in the monastery. On the contrary, as soon as he overcame them, he started writing about them, calling them agonies "so great and so much like hell that no tongue could adequately express them, no pen could describe them, and one who has not himself experienced them could not believe them."[14] Luther blamed them all, of course, on Catholic teachings.

Luther chose the German word *anfechtungen* to describe his mental torment in the monastery. Its approximate meaning is "terrible psychological assaults." He provides a concise account of the nature of these assaults in his commentary on the Letter to the Galatians, which he wrote at age thirty-four.

> When I was a monk, I used to think my salvation was undone. . . . I could not find peace, but was constantly crucified by thoughts such as these: "You have committed this or that sin; you are guilty of envy, impatience . . . all your good works are to no avail."[15]

In describing *anfechtungen*, Luther does not speak of physiological symptoms of anxiety, such as shaking or rapid heartbeat. He does not emphasize depressive symptoms, such as despair or hopelessness. He doesn't complain about being persecuted by others. His whole problem was unwanted thoughts: ideas, images, and urges that bolted into his mind, attacking him, crucifying him. The harder he fought them, the stronger they came back.

Luther endured the severest of scruples, agonizing worries that he had committed a minor sin. "Though I lived as a monk without reproach," Luther tells us, "I felt that I was a sinner before God. I raged with a fierce and troubled conscience. My sinfulness tormented me night and day."[16]

Outwardly, Luther was an ideal monk. In his pious practices, he exceeded even the norm of the Augustinians. Yet his conscience would not rest, despite the fact that he fully realized his fears were unreasonable.

> When I was a monk, I made a great effort to live according to the requirements of the monastic rule. I went to confession frequently, and I performed the assigned penances faithfully. Never the less, my conscience could never achieve certainty but was always in doubt and said: "You have not done this correctly. You

were not contrite enough. You omitted this in your confession." Therefore, the longer I tried to heal my uncertain, weak, and troubled conscience with human traditions, the more uncertain, weak, and troubled I continually made it.[17]

Not only Luther, but also his superiors recognized that his conscience needed to be cured. They told him so in shockingly blunt language. Luther writes: "Sometimes my confessor said to me when I repeatedly discussed silly sins with him, 'You are a fool.'" Even Luther's adviser in the monastery, Father Johannes von Staupitz, a kind and gentle man, became frustrated by Luther's unreasonable worries. Luther recalls that the frustrated Staupitz once cried, "Look here, if you expect Christ to forgive you, come in with something to forgive—parricide, blasphemy, adultery—instead of all these peccadilloes!"[18]

Luther also suffered from tormenting thoughts that he attributed to Satan. In a letter to his father, Luther writes, "The devil has raged against me with incredible contrivings to destroy me, so that I have often wondered whether I was the only man in the whole world whom he was seeking."[19]

The devil would play on Luther's overreached conscience. "When I go to bed," Luther writes, "the Devil is always waiting for me. He begins to plague me. He brings out a catalog of sins. He won't quit and presses me hard and accuses me as a sinner."[20] Sometimes, the devil would insert into Luther's mind terrible and frightful images. They could be painful pictures involving a knife,[21] or "all the kinds of sudden and terrible death ever seen, heard, or read by man."[22] Sometimes the devil would torture Luther with unwanted "sexual" or "angry" thoughts.[23]

One of Satan's favorite tactics was to torment Luther with blasphemous ideas, including the idea that God did not exist. "The devil beleaguers and storms a heart with doubt," Luther writes.[24] "Often he has offered an argument of such weight that I didn't know whether God exists or not."[25] Another of Satan's strategies was to present Luther with Bible verses that filled him with fear. "I shall now confess, the devil caught up with me and plagued me with scripture passages until heaven and earth became too small for me."[26] The worst of these passages was a certain verse from Saint Paul's Letter to the Romans: "These words terrified me," Luther writes, "He who through faith is righteous shall live."[27] To Luther this represented a gut-wrenching accusation: since he was not righteous, he would not live eternally; despite all of his efforts in the monastery, he was destined for perdition.

> I lay captured by the Devil. I was lost in death. My sinfulness tormented me night and day. I fell ever deeper into it. There was nothing good about my life. Sin had taken possession of me. Fear drove me to despair.[28]

Searching for a Cure

Luther never gave up looking for a solution to the tormenting thoughts that hounded him throughout his early monastery years. The Catholic church of his day did, in fact, offer numerous helps for those beset with religious worries. Such problems, after all, were not unusual. The church felt ready to assist its anxious flock.

First of all, an individual could be reassured of God's love and forgiveness through receiving the sacraments, the formal rites of the church that directly transmitted God's grace. There are seven sacraments in the Catholic church. Of these, two are available on a regular basis: Holy Communion and confession. In communion, the priest presents to a believer consecrated bread and wine, and he or she becomes mystically joined to Christ at the moment of consuming them. Nearly all devout Catholics receive some sort of a sense of consolation from participating in this central rite of the church. Luther, however, felt nothing. His anxieties were too great. "After the celebration of Mass," Luther wrote, "I was never able to find rest in my heart."[29]

The sacrament of confession addresses most directly the pangs of a troubled conscience. Here, if anywhere, one would expect that Luther would have received relief from his inner torment. Luther, however, could never be sure either that he had confessed all his sins or that he had been sufficiently repentant. Rather than relieving Luther's agonizing feelings of sinfulness, confessing only stirred them up.

As a result, the sacrament of confession became a particular problem for Luther. He would engage a priest for as long as six hours at a time, splintering even the smallest sin into chains of minute details, all of which he shared. When finally finished, sometimes he would ask if he could start completely over. "No confessor," Luther recalled, "wanted to have anything to do with me."[30] According to one of his fellow monks, Luther was threatened that if he didn't stop his inappropriate behaviors, he would be disciplined for "obstruction of confession."[31]

Another of the church's methods for comforting people anxious about their eternal destiny centered on indulgences. According to Catholic teachings of the day, sins are an individual's responsibility, but goodness can be shared. The church can transfer merits won by its saints to other persons in exchange for the performance of virtuous acts, such as donating to the church or making a pilgrimage. This transfer of credit is called an "indulgence." There is no question that the Catholic church of Luther's day unconscionably abused this practice as a means of raising money. Still, the rite provided genuine consolation to large numbers of people. Not so for Luther. On a trip to Rome at age twenty-seven, Luther sought indulgences for himself and his family through one of the popular rites afforded to pilgrims, climbing Pilate's stairs. Luther ascended the sacred staircase on his hands and knees, kissing each step while repeating a prayer. At the top, however, rather than being consoled, he was overcome by tormenting anxieties. Doubt prevented him from appreciating the indulgences that were his due.

Another mechanism by which the faithful could be reassured of God's grace was the performance of penances, self-punishing acts that were done in the spirit of imitating Jesus in his sufferings. These ranged from lengthy fasts, to self-flagellation, to enduring extremes of cold. Monks, above all, took solace from such practices, generally regarded as iron-clad insurance against loss of salvation.

Luther outperformed all the other monks in his practice of penances. Looking back on his early monastery years, he writes, "Only truly afflicted consciences fasted in earnest. I almost fasted myself to death, for again and again I went for three days without taking a drop of water or a morsel of food."[32] "My body was horribly tormented and exhausted."[33] He also tortured himself with all-night vigils in the freezing cold, refusing to ask for extra clothes or blankets to keep warm. "The frost alone might have killed me. It caused me pain such as I will never inflict on myself again."[34] Yet while a normal monk could rest secure in a life of self-sacrifice, Luther could not. His anxieties prevented him.

Prayer, of course, formed the major part of the daily life of all monks. Most of them, undoubtedly, believed that their prayers for the most part accomplished their aim: a raising of the heart and mind to God. But Luther did not. He prayed and prayed—all of his life he was a great prayer. Yet in his early monastery years, his anxious thoughts prevented him from getting anywhere. He would shut himself in his room and pray for two, even three days at a time, but this would only make his "head split." Often, it appears, he would recite prayers over and over, monotonously, in attempts to keep his anxiety at bay. In his later life, Luther would look back with regret on "all those prayers that I mumbled."[35]

If all else failed, a troubled monk could still find comfort through the guidance of a spiritual director; Johannes Staupitz,

Luther's director throughout his time in the monastery, was a good man. Staupitz, in fact, was the only Catholic priest that Luther trusted and respected his entire life. In those early, troubled years, Staupitz did aid Luther by providing unflagging support, promoting him through the ranks of the Augustinians, and diverting his attention, at times at least, from his obsessive preoccupation with his "sins." But Staupitz did not recognize the true nature and severity of Luther's anxieties. When Luther asked Staupitz whether he had ever experienced trials such as his, Staupitz said he hadn't. When Luther asked whether he understood them, Staupitz admitted that he didn't.

Nothing worked for Luther. "The longer I tried to heal my uncertain, weak, and troubled conscience," he tells us, "the more uncertain, weak, and troubled I continually made it."[36] As the years passed, all that remained "was the stark-naked desire for help." Yet lasting help he could not find. As a result, Luther began to lose hope. "I, Martin Luther, would have killed myself if the light of the Gospel had not come," the great man writes.[37] His life might have been short, but for a fateful decision made by Staupitz that allowed that light to come.

Sola Fide (By Faith Alone)

When Luther was twenty-eight, Staupitz chose to assign him to a nearby university to lecture on the Bible. Having been unable to help Luther himself, Staupitz perhaps hoped that a careful study of scripture might shake the young monk loose from his irrational anxieties. Luther protested that he was not up to the task, but Staupitz was firm. Once set on his new course, Luther immersed himself in Bible study, weighing the meaning of every passage in light of ancient Greek texts and poring over the written commentaries of theologians. In the process, Luther virtually memorized the entirety of scripture.

Finally, sometime around the age of thirty-two, perhaps in the year 1515, Luther had an extraordinary insight, a sudden moment of intuitive understanding that would change his life forever. It occurred when he was studying in his small office in the tower of the Augustinian monastery. He had been given the assignment of preparing a lecture on Saint Paul's Letter to the Romans. He agonized terribly over the task, because it forced him to carefully consider that one verse that had struck terror in his heart for years: "He who through faith is righteous shall live" (Rom. 1:17). Yet, as Luther's eyes now swept over these words, a flash of understanding gleaned from his study of the Greek language transformed their entire meaning.

It was mostly a matter of the interpretation of the word *righteous*. Luther had been "taught to understand that God is righteous and punishes the unrighteous sinner."[38] So he had been "utterly terror-stricken at the sight of Christ the Judge." At times, he had even "hated the righteous God," because no matter how hard he tried, he could not stop himself from thinking sinful thoughts. Now, he saw that *righteousness* could be better translated as "a gift of God" provided to those on whom he chose to confer it. Rather than a demanding judge, God was a kindhearted benefactor to certain people. It did not matter whether they were sinners. All that was important was that they had faith. If they had faith, then God granted them righteousness.[39]

Luther came to see that faith represents primarily a heartfelt belief, or trust, in God's goodness. "This is to behold God in faith," Luther writes, "that you should look upon his fatherly, friendly heart, in which there is no anger nor ungraciousness."[40] Luther had been incapable of overcoming his sense of sinfulness, but faith, by the grace of God, was freely given to him.

Luther was ecstatic over his discovery of the true meaning of righteousness and faith. "Here I felt that I was altogether born again, and had entered paradise itself," he writes.[41] This represented a Copernican revolution in Luther's thought. His worries were entirely recast, reframed, in a new worldview.

59

With this discovery, Luther's anxieties all but vanished. For the rest of his life, he would be guided by the words *sola fide,* "by faith alone." In theological treatises, sermons, and letters of spiritual direction, Luther would return again and again to the insight that had been revealed to him in the tower of the monastery.

The New Martin Luther

After his discovery of *sola fide,* Luther experienced a dozen of the most extraordinary years ever lived. With newfound self-confidence, he poured himself into preaching and writing about his newfound insights. Soon he felt obliged to speak out against a misuse of the Catholic practice of indulgences by Pope Leo X, unpopular in his own day and regarded by many modern historians as an outright scoundrel. Leo X was exploiting the practice by promising complete remission of sins for those who contributed money to the church. Luther posted ninety-five tersely written theses on the door of his church, arguing vociferously against the abuse.

To Luther's surprise, his sharp criticism of indulgences was received enthusiastically by German princes and commoners alike, all of whom were growing weary of sending money to Rome. The ninety-five theses were copied and passed from hand to hand throughout Germany. Luther was treated as a hero. Events unfolded quickly. Luther found more and more faults with his church. Finally, he came to completely refute the authority of the pope, and even to argue that priests were unnecessary. Luther was excommunicated from the Catholic church in 1521. A full-scale, momentous revolt against his old church was under way, and Luther led it single-handedly.

During these great years, his early thirties to mid-forties, Luther's output was astounding. He taught and preached every day, conversed with leading intellectuals throughout Europe, and published on the average a new religious treatise every two weeks. His personality underwent a metamorphosis. He blossomed into a superb speaker and debater, and a tireless, charismatic leader. No longer a guilt-ridden, diffident monk, he raged and poured insults on anyone who disagreed with him. An eyewitness to a theological debate in 1519 described Luther in these words:

> Martin is of middle height, emaciated from worry and study, so that you can almost count the bones through his skin. He is in the vigor of manhood and has a clear, penetrating voice. A perfect forest of words and ideas stands at his command. He is equal to anything.[42]

By age forty-three, Luther had already exceeded the era's normal life span. He was not taking care of himself. He worked nonstop, and he was drinking more beer than was good for him. He now referred to himself as the "fat doctor." Health problems began to pile up. First, a kidney stone almost killed him. After that, he developed chronic indigestion, headaches, chest pains, dizziness, constipation, and agonizing hemorrhoids that made his life miserable. There was an ever-present buzzing in his ears, as well, and an oozing infection of his leg that required frequent draining.

Psychological stresses were also severe at this time—not worries about his own sinfulness, but legitimate concerns about the outcome of his Reformation. The Catholics were mounting a strong intellectual counteroffensive led by Ignatius of Loyola. At the same time, the terrible "Peasants' War" had broken out amongst his own Protestant followers. As if God were showing his wrath, the Black Plague raged through Germany.

At forty-four, Luther sank into a period of severe depression, with low energy, sleep disturbance, and a preoccupation with death. Luther wrote of those who suffer such deep despair: "Unless God comforts them, they must end their own lives because of their despair, their distress, and their inability to bear their grief."[43] Luther recovered from this episode but was never the same. His great years were behind him. Although he continued to forcefully lead the Reformation, there were no more innovative ideas or remarkable achievements.

As Luther aged, unfortunately, he also became more petulant, irritable, and unrestrained. All of the events that Luther admirers would like to forget, including his complicity in the extermination of Anabaptist sects and his publishing of two anti-Semitic works, occurred during the final quarter of his life. Martin Luther died in 1546, at age sixty-two. He had been feeling ill but had agreed to a horseback ride of some distance in order to mitigate a dispute between two landowners. The physical exertion proved too much, and a heart attack, or perhaps a stroke, felled him.

Luther: A Modern Psychiatric Perspective

For more than a decade, Martin Luther suffered from thoughts that flew into his mind and caused him panic. He suffered them every day, perhaps even every waking hour. Whether he thought they were from Satan or from his own diseased conscience, he recognized them as inappropriate. He fought them with all his might, but they did not relent. Clearly, Luther suffered from clinical obsessions.

Compulsions are defined as excessive, repetitive acts that are performed in order to lessen the anxiety of obsessions. Luther confessed for six hours, then asked for more time. He was threatened with corrective action unless he stopped. This was compulsive confessing at its most severe.

Luther's prayers also deserve comment. In his early monastery years, Luther prayed for astonishing periods of time yet never found peace. He tells us that his prayers were often sterile and repetitive. He refers to "mumbled prayers," and words that he repeated "very coldly."[44] Compulsive prayers, as opposed to meaningful prayers, are mere incantations, rote repetitions of words that are used to counter tormenting thoughts. They are common in the present day among highly religious patients with obsessive-compulsive disorder. To me, the weight of the evidence suggests that Luther, too, often prayed compulsively.

Luther's repeated performance of extreme bodily penances also suggests compulsions. In our time, we see young men with obsessive-compulsive disorder who relentlessly, compulsively, pursue body building, sometimes sacrificing their health in order to overcome the tormenting thought that they are weaklings. Luther writes, "By fasting, abstinence, and austerity in the matter of work and clothing I nearly killed myself."[45] Indeed, it seems a wonder that he survived all his penances. As much as he was performing these excessive religious acts in response to fearful thoughts, and not, as is supposed to be the case in the religious life, out of a sincere desire to imitate Christ, then these were also compulsions.

On the basis of what Martin Luther himself tells us about his early monastery experiences, it can reasonably be concluded that he suffered from a textbook case of obsessive-compulsive disorder. Not only did it cause him extraordinary torment and endanger his health, it prevented him from advancing in a monk's most important task: advancing spiritually by growing closer to God. Luther writes, "When I was a monk, I did nothing but waste my time. . . . With all my Masses, with prayers, fasts, vigils, and chastity, I never advanced to the point where I could say that my order and my austere life promoted me heavenward."[46]

Only when one realizes that Luther suffered from obsessive-compulsive disorder do certain puzzling aspects of his life begin to make sense. Luther's superior, Father Staupitz, once threw up his hands and told him bluntly, "I just don't understand you!"[47] Why was Luther misunderstood in the monastery? Anxiety and depression were rampant in the late Renaissance, and Catholic priests were experts at dealing with them. Yet Luther's symptoms seemed baffling to those to whom he unburdened his troubled conscience. Depression and anxiety are not at all illogical; on the contrary, one readily empathizes with those who suffer from their symptoms. Yet obsessions and compulsions are puzzlingly illogical. Indeed, senselessness and irrationality are hallmarks of obsessive-compulsive disorder.

One also wonders why, if the young monk Luther was in such psychological distress, he would have been so quickly advanced in the Augustinian order, and even given a prized teaching position. The answer is that despite his trials, Luther performed excellently in his outward duties. Here is another of the unique qualities of obsessive-compulsive disorder. Freud noted that those who suffer from it "are able to keep their affliction a private matter; concealment is made easier from the fact that they are quite well able to fulfill their duties during a part of the day, once they have devoted a number of hours to their secret doings, hidden from view."[48] People with severe depression, by contrast, are more often severely impaired.

Richard Marius writes more insightfully than any other biographer about many aspects of Luther's psychological struggles. Without an understanding of Luther's obsessive-compulsive disorder, however, he trips up in a crucial matter. He assumes that Luther's tormenting doubts were serious intellectual considerations that Luther brooded over and carefully weighed. Luther, according to Marius, was "swept along by one of the great recurring waves of skepticism in human history, doubts that God exists at all and that he can or will raise the dead." For Luther, he concludes, "faith and the most radical kind of doubt dwelt intertwined together until the end of his days."[49] What Luther himself reports, however, does not support this interpretation. In his writings, Luther's doubts about God's existence take the form of startling intrusions into his consciousness, ideas so foreign and so threatening to him that he attributes them to Satan. As tormenting as these thoughts were, they were superficial, on-the-wing, not considerations to be pondered. Luther was too terrified of these intrusive thoughts to ever consider them seriously; the minute they occurred he did everything in his power to fight them off. This battle in the mind is the hallmark of a clinical obsession.

It may also be noted that our modern understanding of the clinical symptoms of obsessive-compulsive disorder allows us to correct an error that was made by the two psychiatrists who wrote influential biographies on Luther in the twentieth century. Luther wrote that he frequently felt Satan putting scandalous thoughts into his mind, and that sometimes he would even scream back at Satan to stop bothering him. On the basis of such reports, both Reiter and Erikson concluded that Luther was at times delusional. It has since been demonstrated, however, that people who suffer from blasphemous, intrusive thoughts often attribute them to Satan, and that, in the context of many religious cultures, such a belief does not constitute a loss of contact with reality. Rather, what it indicates is OCD.

Did Martin Luther suffer from a second psychiatric disorder? We know that in the present day the occurrence of severe obsessive-compulsive disorder is associated with an increased risk of developing a number of other disorders, including bipolar disorder, panic, and major depression.

Whether Luther may have had bipolar disorder is an intriguing possibility. Psychiatrists tend to be drawn to it, because bipolar individuals often exhibit, as Luther did, exceptional productivity in their work and extreme volatility in their personality. The diagnosis of bipolar disorder, however, requires alternating mood states. Classically, a person will have a grandiose mood and tireless energy for a few weeks, followed by a more lengthy period of withdrawal and depression. Luther, however, does not appear to have suffered from striking alternations in mood. In his monastery years, he was in a constant state of anxiety. In his great years, he was continually productive. In his later years, he appears to have been mostly depressed. A strong case cannot be made for bipolar disorder.

One might also wonder, given the constant anxiety that he endured, whether Luther suffered from panic disorder, a syndrome that is characterized by repeated attacks of adrenaline-induced anxiety symptoms, such as rapid heartbeat, shortness of breath, chest pains, dizziness, numbness, and nausea. Luther describes two incidents in his life when he became temporarily disabled by anxiety symptoms: at age twenty-one when he was knocked to the ground by lightning, and two years later when he led his first worship service as a priest. In the latter incident, he suddenly became terrified and weak, resuming his duties only after being prodded by his prior, who stood beside him. Yet neither episode represents a clear panic attack; furthermore, he apparently suffered no other severe occurrences of this nature. The diagnosis of panic disorder also cannot be made.

"Major depression" is a clinical syndrome of low mood, withdrawal, and loss of sleep and appetite. Two-thirds of people with severe obsessive-compulsive disorder develop the malady at some point during their lives. Luther, it strongly appears, did suffer from one or more episodes of major depression during his later life. The profound depression that he experienced at age forty-four lasted almost a year. From his description, it amounted to the severe form of major depression called "melancholia," in which a person's entire sense of awareness becomes distorted, colored by a relentlessly black mood. Luther writes,

> Those who experience sadness of spirit, to them all creatures appear changed. Even when they speak with people who they know and in turn hear them, the very sound of their speech seems different, their looks appear changed, and everything becomes black and horrible where ever they turn their eyes.[50]

In sum, it would appear that Luther suffered from two clearly discernible psychiatric disorders during his life: obsessive-compulsive disorder and major depressive disorder. Regarding his depressions, nothing positive can be said. They probably contributed to the poor judgment he showed in his later years. Luther's experience with obsessive-compulsive disorder, however, was different. Striking him in the prime of his life, it played the role of a catalyst: it stimulated him to his great theological discovery, *sola fide,* which served to make him a new man.

The Riddle of *Sola Fide*

Herein lies a puzzle. Why was Luther driven to find such a radical solution to his anxieties? Its revolutionary nature cannot be overemphasized. What *sola fide* implied was that the Catholic church had no automatic monopoly as keeper of the sacraments nor was it the single, preordained instrument by which people come to God. Luther never doubted the importance of the church as a community of faith, but he insisted it could go astray and require correction by the Word. The first and most important relation of the people with God was through the Word known in Christ and scripture, not the people with the church.

Luther, it should be noted, was not by nature a revolutionary. He was, like most OCD sufferers, an extremely loyal individual. For decades he suffered pangs of guilt for disappointing his parents by entering the monastery. When he finally married at age forty-one, Luther says that he did it, among other reasons, in order to finally please his father. At times, he had similar feelings about his rebellion against Catholicism. At age thirty-seven, his theological writings already condemned by Rome and his Reformation well under way, he begins a letter to the pope with these surprising words, "Most blessed father, in all the controversies of the past three years I have ever been mindful of you."[51] Luther did not finally remove his monastic garb until age forty-one, three years after being officially excommunicated.

One might think that Luther, an extremely bright and thoughtful man who was in need of a new approach to God that would lessen his anxieties, could have adopted any one of a number of different theological viewpoints that were present within the Catholic church of his day. A mystical tradition had flowered that promoted union with God through contemplative prayer, and which deemphasized the performance of rituals and penances. Luther was familiar with the writings of the medieval mystics, Tauler in particular; and his spiritual director, Father Staupitz, actually leaned in this direction. Another possible approach that Luther was well aware of, and which he might have found helpful for his tormenting anxieties, was the humanistic theology championed by Erasmus of Rotterdam, the leading Catholic intellectual of his day. It stressed the importance of living a simple Christ-like life, and of not bothering with difficult theological questions.

Yet Luther was not drawn to any of these approaches. It was only *sola fide*, and no other theological consideration, that captured him. And he would not budge an iota on the full implications of this doctrine. Even while Luther was rebelling against certain doctrines in Catholicism, moderates such as Erasmus were strongly challenging the Vatican on the same issues. They attempted to find common theological ground with Luther. But Luther would have no part of it.

Luther's followers have a single answer to why he was drawn to *sola fide* and stuck to it so vociferously: it was the truth revealed to him by God. That may be, but is there a psychological explanation? Recent scientific research suggests that *sola fide* represented a specific and powerful cure for Luther's obsessions and compulsions, perhaps the best that he could possibly have found. Before looking at that research, we will examine the lives of two other great Christians, lives that were remarkably similar, in important ways, to Luther's: John Bunyan and Saint Thérèse of Lisieux.

| 4 |

John Bunyan
The Pilgrim's Fears of Hellfire

One of the most intriguing facts about the Renaissance epidemic of religious obsessions and compulsions is that Luther's Reformation did little to slow it down. Luther eliminated mandatory confession in the church that he founded, and he advocated a theology that was supposed to be based on trust rather than fear. For Luther—and one would think for many other Christians as well—these were effective anti-obsession measures. Yet large numbers of Protestants still came to be tormented by overwhelming fears for their salvation.

Many lived in terror of committing the "unpardonable sin" mentioned in the Bible, which, once committed, removes all chance of eternal salvation. Instead of repeated confessing, Protestants typically would spend hours making devotions, reading and rereading certain Bible passages, and pestering their ministers for reassurance on the states of their souls.

The dangers of Protestant scrupulosity were described in detail a century after Luther's death by the most distinguished

Anglican of the seventeenth century, Bishop Jeremy Taylor. In *The Rule of Conscience*, Taylor devotes an entire chapter to the "timorous and fearful people" who "accuse themselves without reason, and repent when they have not sinned." Many of them suffered from what we now recognize as obsessive-compulsive disorder. As an example, Taylor describes the interesting case of William of Oseney, a devout Anglican, who developed compulsions to read devotional material.

> William resolved to spend three hours every day reading religious books. In short time he began to think that now he was to spend six hours every day in reading those books, because he had now read them over six times. He presently considered that by the proportion of this scruple he must be tied to twelve hours every day. . . . His thoughts revolved in a restless circle, and made him fear he knew not what. . . . He was sure this scruple was unreasonable, [but] seeking for remedy he grew infinitely worse.

Taylor held his church responsible for failing to provide a remedy. "In this case," he notes wryly, "the religion is not so great as the affliction."[1]

Obsessional fears appear to have been a particular problem for the English Puritans, a diverse group, formed in the sixteenth century, who believed that the Anglican church had not been sufficiently "purified" from Catholic heresy. Puritans drew their inspiration from the austere French Reformer John Calvin. They were known for their intense self-discipline and contempt for worldly delights. The movement flourished in the seventeenth century, attracting followers including Oliver Cromwell, Lord Protector of England during Bunyan's early years, and the greatest poet of the age, John Milton, author of *Paradise Lost*.

Hawthorne's popular Puritan tale *The Scarlet Letter* has accustomed us to believe that Puritans were obsessed with sin, and to some extent this appears to have been true. All of Puritan theology converged on the importance of divine judgment, God's fearsome decision regarding each person's eternal destiny. In order to be certain that God judged them favorably, Puritans aimed to live spotless lives. "The whole object of the Puritan's existence," as noted by historian Alan Simpson, "was warfare against sin."[2] For people with tender consciences, the price paid was an extreme degree of anxiety.

The Puritan writer Richard Baxter, in his well-known *Christian Directory*, observed the malady that developed. In a description that could easily have been taken from a Catholic penitential manual of the thirteenth century, he notes the fate of those Puritans with too delicate a conscience.

> They are endless with their scruples, afraid lest they sin in every word and thought. They ensnare themselves in many vows, touch not, taste not, handle not; and in self imposed tasks, spending so many hours in this or that act of devotion. They think against their will that which they are most afraid of thinking. They are troubled with hideous blasphemous temptations, against God or Christ, or the scripture.[3]

"The very pain of their fears," Baxter observes, "draws their thoughts to what they fear." Here, the seventeenth-century author fixes squarely on the psychological paradox that has been proven to exacerbate obsessions: the harder one resists a tormenting a thought, the stronger it returns. Baxter also insightfully describes the personalities of such individuals: "No man can be less willing of any sin," he writes, "than these poor souls." There is no difficulty recognizing the disorder Baxter depicts.

A century ago, William James referred to "patient Bunyan . . . sensitive of conscience to a diseased degree, beset by doubts, fears, and insistent ideas."[4] In the present day, Bunyan's case is often cited as a classic example of obsessive-compulsive disorder. Indeed, Bunyan's descriptions of his agonizing obsessions and compulsions represent our best historical example of the disorder.

John Bunyan, somewhat amazingly, is not well known today. His name was a household word from the seventeenth century to the twentieth. George Bernard Shaw called Bunyan "England's greatest prose writer," and Rudyard Kipling referred to him as the "father of the novel." Bunyan's fame rests largely on a single masterpiece that he wrote in jail at a time when the Puritans were being persecuted, *The Pilgrim's Progress*. It is about a man named Christian who overcomes many extreme perils on a journey to find his salvation. On a veiled psychological level, it is the story of how Bunyan himself overcame his own psychological struggles.

The appealing religious message of *The Pilgrim's Progress*, even more than its literary value, has made it the most important book after the Bible for centuries of Protestant Christians. Catholics, with a few necessary deletions, have adopted the book, as well. Its remarkable influence can be measured by the fact that it has been translated into more than two hundred languages and is said, even now, to be the second most-published book in history.

Another book written by Bunyan is less well known but even more important for an understanding of the man. His spiritual autobiography, *Grace Abounding to the Chief of Sinners*, contains almost all that is known about the facts of Bunyan's life. More than that, Bunyan refers to it as the "unfolding of my secret things." It is a truly remarkable self-analysis that allows his mental state to be understood in a manner that is more complete, perhaps, than that of any other major religious figure in history. It is the most fearless account of obsessive-compulsive disorder ever composed.

Young John Bunyan

Bunyan's childhood was a difficult one. He was born in 1628 near the village of Bedford, England. His father, a struggling tinker, a mender of pots and pans, owned nothing more than a house so small that it was exempt from taxes. Bunyan attended a school for poor men's children. During his youth, he lost both his mother and his sister to epidemics of infectious disease that raged through the country. Not only epidemics of disease, but civil war racked England during these years. "The third, fourth, and fifth decades of the seventeenth century," writes historian Peter Bowden, "were probably among the most terrible years through which the country has ever passed; . . . many experienced extreme poverty, living desperately from one meager harvest to the next."[5]

It has been suggested that people at the mercy of uncontrollable and hostile forces seek comfort from religion. This tumultuous period in England was, in fact, marked by extraordinary religious fervor. The state-run Anglican church was tottering toward ruin, and in its absence there raged a free-for-all battle for people's souls. Itinerant preachers from radical Protestant sects with long-forgotten names such as "Ranters" and "Muggletonians" came, one after another, to the squares of small towns, drawing thousands of people and stirring up great excitement.

It has also been proposed that the battered-down are drawn to an especially harsh view of God. This outlook prevailed in most of the sects popular during Bunyan's time. God, it was widely believed, had chosen his "elect" from the beginning; everyone else was damned. The poor had to suffer here on earth in order to receive their reward in heaven. Life was a trial to be lived through. Bunyan's mother was a Puritan, and he was raised according to this severe outlook.

Bunyan spends a slim two pages in *Grace Abounding* describing his early years. This is sufficient, however, to glimpse how he adapted to such an environment. "Even in my childhood the Lord did scare and affright me with fearful dreams, and did terrify me with dreadful visions," Bunyan writes. "I was greatly afflicted and troubled with the thoughts of the Day of Judgment, and should tremble at the thoughts of the fearful torments of hell-fire."[6] Biographer G. B. Harrison provides a description of Bunyan as a child: "a highly sensitive, over strung boy who wilted visibly before the lurid suggestions of what awaited the sinner in another world."[7]

As an adolescent, Bunyan discovered a way to deal with his timid and guilt-prone temperament. He rebelled. "I could not let go my sins," Bunyan writes. "[I decided] that I might be a tormentor, rather than tormented myself." Accordingly, he turned into a rambunctious adolescent. "I had few equals," Bunyan says, "for cursing, swearing, lying and blaspheming. . . . I was the very ring-leader of all the youth that kept me company, into all manner of vice and ungodliness."[8]

At age fifteen, Bunyan left home and joined the mutinous Parliamentarian army, which aimed at overthrowing the rule of monarchy in England. In his autobiography he tells us next to nothing about his years as a soldier. Apparently, he suffered no major psychological problems, and five years later he returned to Bedford to take up his father's trade. He soon married, and started a family. Then he was struck by acute distress.

For the next six to seven years, agonizing fears would "dart" into Bunyan's mind, "bolt" upon him, and "assault" his soul. "Floods of blasphemies" would be "poured" upon him until they "drowned and overflowed" all other thoughts. Bunyan developed obsessional fears that were, it seems, even worse than Luther's.

Like Luther, Bunyan fought his disorder alone. He found no others who suffered from his condition. As observed by biographer W. Hale White, "the Puritans, for the most part, sat in their shops and quietly went about their business untroubled by their creed."[9] Those who were troubled and did develop obsessions and compulsions, as in all ages and times, tended to keep their problem a secret.

The whole of Bunyan's agonizing struggle with obsessive-compulsive disorder is laid bare in *Grace Abounding*. More than half of its pages contain remarkably full and vivid descriptions of a most extraordinary and varied taxonomy of obsessions and compulsions. Bunyan wrote the book about a decade after he overcame his affliction; it is, therefore, as put by one biographer, "a retrospective account of his emotional disturbance from a position of psychic health."[10] Bunyan sagely acknowledges to the reader the apparent absurdity of the tormenting thoughts he describes, providing a poignant motto that is suitable for obsessive-compulsive disorder sufferers of all eras. "These things may seem ridiculous to others," he observes, "even as ridiculous as they were in themselves, but to me they were the most tormenting cogitations."[11]

The Most Tormenting Cogitations

Clinical obsessions struck John Bunyan at the age of twenty-one or twenty-two, first with a recurrence of the same anxieties that he had suffered in childhood. "I was in the midst of a game," Bunyan writes in *Grace Abounding*, when "a voice did suddenly dart from heaven into my soul which said, 'Wilt thou leave thy sins, and go to heaven? Or have thy sins, and go to hell?'" Bunyan "looked up to heaven," and with his "eyes of understanding," he saw Jesus "hotly displeased, and as if he did severely threaten me with some grievous punishment."[12]

Bunyan attempted to deal with the resulting fear by using the same strategy that had worked for him a decade before. "I had as good be damned for many sins, as to be damned for a few," he reasoned. Once again he resumed the role of a troublemaker. This time, however, the approach failed: his intrusive fears of sinfulness would not relent. Bunyan then tried a different approach: He joined a church. "I fell to some outward reformation, both in my words and life," he relates. His neighbors started to look up to him. He felt better. "I thought I pleased

75

God as well as any man in England."[13] This conversion quelled his fears for about a year.

Obsessional doubts then began to plague him more severely than ever. Sometimes they took the form of "questions against the very being of God,"[14] similar to the questions of God's existence that had tormented Luther. Even more agonizing were Bunyan's doubts about his salvation.

> I began to find my soul to be assaulted with fresh doubts. . . . How can you tell you are elected? And what if you should not? . . . This question did so offend and discourage me, that it was sometimes as if the very strength of my body had been taken away by the force and power thereof. . . . By these things I was driven to my wits' end.[15]

As time passed, not only doubts, but the worst sorts of blasphemous thoughts afflicted him, thoughts so profane that, Bunyan warns us, "I may not, at this time, dare utter [these thoughts], neither by word nor pen."[16] One might guess that these were violent or sexual obsessions. He describes their terror.

> A very great storm came upon me . . . whole floods of blasphemies were poured upon my spirit, to my great confusion and astonishment. These suggestions did make such a seizure upon my spirit, and did so over-weigh my heart, both with their number, continuance, and fiery force, that I felt as if there were nothing else but these from morning to night.[17]

Eventually, Bible verses became the most troublesome obsessions of all. Certain passages, such as "It is a fearful thing to fall into the hands of the living God" (Heb. 10:31 KJV), turned into overpowering fears that tortured Bunyan. To counter them, he would read and reread other verses that gave him comfort, such as "I have blotted out . . . thy transgressions" (Isa. 44:22 KJV). He compulsively repeated such verses until they lost the power to console him. Then, gripped again by terrifying dread, he would desperately search for yet another passage to allay his torment. For hours at a time, as biographer Christopher Hill notes, Bunyan "pored in terrifying isolation over his Bible."[18] Dozens of conflicting verses flew through his mind. Fully twenty pages of *Grace Abounding* are devoted to a colossal, obsessional battle of Bible verses.

Of all the Bible-based obsessions that Bunyan suffered, the worst was a tormenting thought to "sell Christ." This obsession struck when Bunyan was reading the Old Testament passage about a man named Esau who had chosen to sell his inheritance (Gen. 25:33). In Bunyan's interpretation, what Esau had actually sold was his salvation. The thought suddenly burst into Bunyan's mind that he himself should "sell Christ." This thought drove him to conclude that he had finally committed an unforgivable sin, because, he tells us, "My sin was point blank against my savior."[19]

The "sell Christ" obsession struck Bunyan after he had joined a Baptist sect with Puritan leanings and had, for a short while, experienced peace. He was twenty-six. The "wicked suggestion" became a constant torment. Nothing "in the least did shake or abate the continuation of force and strength thereof," Bunyan writes, "for it did always in almost whatever I thought, intermix itself." The phrase would run in his mind, "as fast as a man could speak."

> I could neither eat my food, stoop for a pin, chop a stick, or cast mine eye to look on this or that, but still the temptation would come, "Sell Christ for this, or sell Christ for that; sell him, sell him." Sometimes it would run in my thoughts not so little as a hundred times together, sell him, sell him, sell him . . .[20]

In response, Bunyan performed equally endless compulsions. Each time "sell Christ" would come to his mind, he would frantically repeat, as a sort of mantra, "I will not, I will not, I will not, I will not, no not for thousands, thousands, thousands of worlds." He kept this up, he tell us, "even until I was almost out of breath."[21]

To make matters worse, Bunyan relates, "the tempter would make me believe I had consented to sell Christ." Then, he writes, he would be "tortured as on a rack for whole days together."[22] The thought that he had consented to this terrible blasphemy represented an add-on obsession that increased his torment by a quantum jump. Such a cascading of obsessions, one after another, each magnifying torment, occurs frequently in obsessive-compulsive disorder. It drove Bunyan to perform new compulsions that were even more complicated and laborious.

> This temptation did put me to such scares . . . that by the very force of my mind in laboring to gainsay and resist this wickedness, my very body also would be put into action or motion, by way of pushing or thrusting with my hands or elbows.[23]

One can imagine Bunyan pacing furiously back and forth, breathlessly intoning "I will not," punching into the air with his hands and elbows. This is the obsessive-compulsive disorder battle at its most spectacular. Bunyan was truly besieged.

Most present-day obsessive-compulsive disorder sufferers cannot easily relate to Bunyan's extraordinary religious obsessions. Yet he also describes a number of other symptoms that today's sufferers can readily understand. One of my patients, for instance, makes a dash for the door when struck by an obsession of imminent catastrophe. Bunyan provides an enthralling account of a similar occurrence when an improbable series of obsessions struck him one day at church.

> I began to think, what if one of those bells should fall? Then I chose to stand under a main beam . . . thinking there I might stand safe; but then I thought again, should the bell fall with a swing, it might first hit the wall, and then rebounding upon me, might kill me. . . . This made me stand in the steeple door . . . but then it came into my head, what if the steeple itself should

fall? And this thought [did] so shake my mind, that I durst not stand at the steeple door any longer, but was forced to fly, for fear it should fall upon my head.[24]

Other of Bunyan's obsessions involved urges to yell profanities. I once treated a student whose jaws ached for a week from constantly clenching her teeth in order to keep from blurting out obscenities during cheerleading tryouts. Bunyan describes a similar episode.

The tempter [would] provoke me to desire to sin . . . if it were to be committed by speaking of such a word, then I have been as if my mouth would have spoken that word whether I would or no; and in so strong a measure was this temptation upon me, that often I have been ready to clap my hand under my chin, to hold my mouth from opening; and to that end also I have had thoughts at other times to leap with my head downward into some muck-hill hole or other, to keep my mouth from speaking.[25]

A very common symptom of obsessive-compulsive disorder in the present age is the urge to commit repulsive violent and sexual acts. Bunyan suffered from these, as well. "Lusts and corruptions would strongly put forth themselves within me," he writes, "in wicked thoughts and desires."[26] One particularly troublesome obsession that occurred while Bunyan was performing his ministerial duties was the thought to kill those to whom he was giving the bread of communion. "I had not been long a partaker at the [sacrament]," Bunyan writes, "but such fierce and sad temptations did attend me . . . to wish some deadly thing to those that then did eat thereof."[27]

Panic attacks, severe episodes of anxiety accompanied by physical symptoms such as shaking, chest pains, nausea, and rapid heartbeat, occur in up to one-third of obsessive-compulsive disorder sufferers in the present day. Bunyan relates an apparent panic attack that he suffered on the heels of a particularly bad obsession.

> I struck into a very great trembling. . . . I could for whole days
> together feel my very body as well as my mind to shake and totter
> under the sense of the dreadful judgment of God. . . . I felt also such
> a clogging and heat at my stomach by reason of this my terror,
> that it was as if my breast-bone would have split in sunder.[28]

Like many present-day obsessive-compulsive disorder sufferers, Bunyan sometimes thought that he was going crazy. "Now I thought surely I am possessed of the devil," he writes; "at other times again I thought I should be bereft of my wits."[29] Yet despite his self-doubts and severe torment, Bunyan was able to raise his family during this time, and to function effectively both as a tinker and a minister. This too is an irony well understood by those who suffer from the disorder in the present day. They can suffer extreme agony for hours each day, yet still manage to do life's work.

Above all, present-day sufferers may relate to Bunyan's matchless descriptions of the relentless mental battle that is the hallmark of obsessive-compulsive disorder. Only a person who knows the disorder firsthand can really appreciate how Bunyan's obsessions "dart" into his mind, "bolt" upon him, "assault" and "break in" to his soul, "strangely snatching" him away. How they "return upon" him, and "stick with" him, "running" in his mind "as fast as a man can speak." How they "fiercely assault" him like "a mighty whirlwind . . . as if racked upon the wheel." How, in response to these tormentors, he "kicked" and "screamed"; he "resisted" by the "force of his mind." And how, neither his "dislike of the thoughts, nor yet any desire and endeavor to resist them, did in the least shake or abate their continuation or force and strength."

Surmounting the Crisis

On the title page of *Grace Abounding*, Bunyan announces that his book is "published for the support of the weak and tempted people of God." He had good news to share with them: "How the Lord did deliver [me] from all guilt and terror." More than just a textbook of obsessions and compulsions, his autobiography is a treatment manual. Bunyan possessed an astounding capacity for introspective analysis, but he was a man of action as well. In his early years he had developed an aggressive strategy for dealing with his fragile psychology. When his tormenting fears reoccurred in his early twenties, he did not sit idly by.

He made at least one attempt to seek help. Mustering courage, he approached "an ancient Christian" whom he held in high esteem, and confided his worst blasphemous thoughts and tormenting doubts. He even shared his deepest fear, that he had lost his salvation: "I told him," Bunyan writes, "that I was afraid that I had sinned the sin against the Holy Ghost." The reply of his counselor is remarkable, to say the least. "He told me," Bunyan relates, that "he thought so, too."[30] (This may be the worst advice for obsessions ever recorded—the equivalent of telling a compulsive hand washer, "Yes, your hands probably are contaminated"!) Bunyan comments wryly: "I had but cold comfort."

Not surprisingly, given the advice he had received and the forcefulness of his personality, Bunyan set out to conquer his disorder on his own. Although discerning a time line for the events in *Grace Abounding* is difficult, it appears that he rapidly progressed in finding ways to productively deal with his ailment during the last one to two years that he suffered severely.

Bunyan's first major victory over obsessions came when he was able to view them in a more reflective, rational light. Whereas before, Bunyan tells us, "I thought they would destroy me . . . I dared scarce cast mine eye [on them]." Now, he says, "I began to take some measure of encouragement, to come close to them, to read them and consider them, and to weigh their scope and tendency." The result of his new outlook was immediate: "I found their visage changed; for they looked not so grimly on me as before."[31]

Bunyan then decided to try a bold experiment. It happened on a day when was alternately hounded and then comforted by Bible passages. "I was in diverse frames of spirit," Bunyan writes, "according to the nature of the several scriptures that came in upon my mind. If this of grace, then I was quiet," he writes, "but if that of Esau, then tormented." He decided to invite both of the scriptures to come into his mind. "I wondered which of them would get the better of me," he writes. Soon the result came: "both bolted upon me, and did work and struggle strangely in me for a while. At last, that about Esau's birthright began to wax weak, and withdraw, and vanish; and this about the sufficiency of grace prevailed, with peace and joy."[32]

These strategies, quite remarkable, mirrored the treatment Bunyan might have been given in the present day by a cognitive-behavioral therapist. And yet, they were not sufficient. To Bunyan's great consternation, tormenting thoughts soon began again to afflict him. Some of his worst struggles, in fact, occurred in the last months before he finally claimed full victory over the disorder.

Bunyan could now view his obsessions more rationally, but his newly found reliance on logic seemed to drive him relentlessly into a well-known irony of Calvinistic theology: the elect could feel secure, because they had been chosen from the beginning of time; yet there was no certain means for an individual to tell whether or not he had, in fact, been chosen as one of the elect. Interestingly, Calvin himself had anticipated the anxieties that this concern could cause. His advice was not to delve too deeply into the matter of election, for the works of the Lord are a "deep abyss." This advice worked for the majority of Puritans, apparently; but not for Bunyan and others like him who trembled "under the sense of the dreadful judgment of God." "When I cried for mercy," Bunyan remembers, "this would come, 'tis too late'"[33]

At this time, Bunyan was profoundly discouraged. It was probably the lowest point of his life. He explains the theological irons that gripped him. "I saw that I wanted a perfect righteousness, and that this righteousness was nowhere to be found but in the person of Jesus Christ."[34] (This idea reflects standard Calvinistic theology: Bunyan was a hopeless sinner, and he could only be "presented" to God on the basis of Christ's moral perfection.) And yet, because of his blasphemous obsessions, Bunyan concluded, finally, "I was lost . . . I had not Christ."[35] He was, thus, by his own reasoning, completely cut off from any relationship with God, and from any chance of salvation.

A series of extraordinary occurrences soon rescued Bunyan once and for all from his dismal state. From a psychological standpoint, it was as if, after rationality had failed, his unconscious mind stepped in to heal him. Bunyan experienced a string of therapeutic religious visions. In the first, he received what he took to be a reassurance that Jesus himself would intercede on his behalf and take his place on the judgment seat.

> One day as I was passing in a field, with some dashes on my conscience, fearing lest yet all was not yet right, I saw with the eyes of my soul Jesus Christ at God's right hand, as my righteousness. My righteousness was Jesus Christ himself. . . . now I could look from myself to him.[36]

No longer did Bunyan feel cut off from Christ. "I was loosed from my affliction and irons," Bunyan writes. "My temptations also fled away . . . those dreadful scriptures of God left off to trouble me."[37]

Bunyan even began to have mystical experiences of God, something far removed from the Calvinistic and Puritan norm.[38] "The Lord did also lead me into the mystery of union with his son, that I was joined to him," he tells us. "Now could I see myself in heaven and earth at once." Bunyan describes his final obsessive-compulsive disorder crisis. "There fell upon me a great cloud of darkness . . . I suddenly felt this word to sound in my heart, 'I must go to Jesus' . . . the most blessed things of heaven were set within my view."[39]

In accepting his visions, Bunyan found a new way to view God that, at least in regard to obsessive-compulsive disorder, proved to be his salvation. From the time of this discovery to the end of his life at age sixty, Bunyan's obsessive-compulsive disorder was manageable. Like most people with severe obsessions and compulsions, he was never completely rid of his symptoms. He tells us, for instance, that in his later years he continued to suffer occasional obsessive urges to blurt out obscenities while preaching.[40] But during these years, his fame grew as a preacher, he wrote prolifically, and, best of all, he appears to have enjoyed his life.

Bunyan in Perspective

Bunyan's major biographers have offered many theories to account for his mental turmoil. Astonishingly, however, none of them involve obsessive-compulsive disorder. Bunyan biographer Roger Sharrock, a professor of English at the University of Durham, states that Bunyan's "religious development can easily be studied as a psychiatric case-history showing a progress from severe maladjustment (accompanied by hallucinations and paranoiac symptoms) to a successful integration of the personality."[41] Monica Furlong, in her popular biography *Puritan's Progress*, states that "Bunyan was gripped with paranoid fears."[42] Gordon Wakefield, in *Bunyan the Christian*, noting a possible relationship between religious experience and schizophrenia, wonders whether Bunyan was "on the verge of insanity."[43]

Other biographers have labeled Bunyan's psychological struggle as a type of depression. R. H. Thouless, writing from a medical perspective in 1923, sees Bunyan as a "melancholiac" and notes that many of his symptoms were identical to those he observed among acutely depressed patients in mental hospitals.[44] Ernst Bacon, a Puritan himself, reduces Bunyan's troubled years to "a period of introspection and retrospection . . . an unsettled state."[45]

Still other biographers have proposed that Bunyan suffered a "neurosis" that can be explained only in light of Freudian assumptions. The psychoanalytic interpretation of Bunyan's struggles is most clearly spelled out by W. N. Evans in a 1943 study. According to Evans, Bunyan remained fixed at an infantile, anal phase of development, which caused him to be preoccupied with sadistic fantasies.[46]

All Bunyan biographers agree that he suffered a lengthy period of severe psychiatric symptoms and then was cured. Yet all of them draw conclusions that are based on outdated psychiatric concepts. Bunyan was clearly not psychotic. His "hallucinations," like Luther's, would not be diagnosed as such today. Nor was he "paranoid" in the modern clinical sense; his extreme fear of God's wrath was shared by other members of his church. Bunyan certainly was depressed at times, but he did not undergo, as Luther had, a severe and lengthy melancholic episode. As for Freudian, psychoanalytic formulations for obsessive-compulsive disorder, they have by now been completely discredited.

Furlong speculates in her 1975 biography on how a "modern" psychiatrist might treat Bunyan: "He might have lived out the acute phase of his paranoia in a mental hospital. . . . He would have been regarded, and so have come to regard himself, as a sick man, even as a mad man."[47] Psychiatry had little to offer obsessive-compulsive disorder sufferers in 1975, but things weren't as bad as Furlong suggests. No competent doctor would have diagnosed him as paranoid, and he certainly would not have been kept in a mental hospital. Like most people who suffer even severe cases of the disorder, Bunyan was able to function amazingly well in day-to-day life even when his disorder was at its worst. Even then Bunyan's case would have been recognized by most psychiatrists as classic obsessive-compulsive disorder.

Deciphering *The Pilgrim's Progress*

The part played by obsessive-compulsive disorder in shaping *The Pilgrim's Progress* has yet to be noted by scholars. Bunyan composed his masterpiece about a decade after he completed *Grace Abounding*. At the time he wrote the first book, his "tormenting cogitations" were still relatively fresh and haunting. In the later work, he was able to take a more distanced perspective on his agonizing disorder.

One may speculate that Bunyan reflected deeply on how to present the life-saving truth that he had described earlier in a different manner, one that could be grasped by everyone. The solution he found, as noted by Roger Sharrock, was "to translate his own spiritual odyssey into an allegory."[48] Bunyan tells us that he wrote *The Pilgrim's Progress* "in the similitude of a dream." He stresses that although the tale is a fantasy, its message is very real: "This book will direct thee to the Holy Land . . . if thou wilt its directions understand."[49]

The Pilgrim's Progress begins with the description of a man named Christian who has left behind his family and all his worldly possessions in order to begin a journey to the Celestial City. "I dreamed," Bunyan famously writes, "and behold I saw a man, clothed in rags, standing in a certain place, a book in his hand, and a great burden upon his back." Christian's is a surreal journey, as one would expect in a dream. Along the way, he is forced to deal with a multitude of fantastic perils, from a dangerous territory called the Slough of Despond to the Valleys of Humiliation and of the Shadow of Death. He is arrested in a town called Vanity Fair, and subsequently imprisoned in a castle owned by a giant whose name is Despair. Escaping, he reaches the River of Death, which he finally crosses, gaining entrance to the Celestial City.

Close brushes with death are interspersed with long conversations between Christian and fellow travelers. This pilgrim, we find, is much more optimistic and outgoing than the one described in *Grace Abounding*. He enjoys talking and bantering. Although his conversations are invariably weighty, and reveal great discrepancies between his beliefs and those of almost everyone else, they are friendly and even cheerful. The tone of the book is thus strangely in conflict with its message, for in the end, only one individual besides Christian finally reaches the Celestial City. Most of the others, one presumes, go to hell. Consistent with the dream premise, nothing seems to matter except what happens to Christian.

The perils that Christian encounters are metaphors for the trials and temptations Bunyan saw as faced by all Christians. Some represent standard themes, such as the importance of humility and, especially, the need to forsake worldly pleasures. The crucial challenges that Christian faces, however, all involve matters of faith. In these struggles with doubt and blasphemy, *The Pilgrim's Progress* mirrors *Grace Abounding*.

At the beginning of his journey, Christian takes the advice of a man called Worldly Wiseman and walks along a path overshadowed by an ominous mountain. He becomes terrified "lest it should fall on [his] head."[50] A man named Evangelist appears, who explains that the mountain, called "Sinai," is very dangerous, indeed. It falls on the heads of those who choose a legalistic path to their salvation. Christian is directed another way.

Not long after, he finds himself walking at night along an "exceedingly narrow pathway," when a "fiend" steps up behind him and "whisperingly" suggests many grievous blasphemies to him. Christian makes the mistake of assuming that these thoughts come from his own mind. After much turmoil and prayer, he sees that the blasphemies actually come from Satan, and he is comforted by God's presence.

Further along in the journey, Christian is thrown into the dungeon of a place called the Doubting Castle. He escapes execution only when he finally remembers, after a night of prayer, that he has the key to the dungeon door right in his pocket. It is called The Promise. "It will," Christian remembers, "open

87

any lock in the Doubting Castle."[51] The Promise could be easily recognized by Bunyan's readers as Christ's assurance to the faithful that he would intercede on their behalf.

Christian's ultimate trial is crossing the hazardous river that lies in front of the Celestial City, a waterway that has the unusual property of being "deeper or shallower, as you believe in the King."[52] Here is the final test for all Christians: How strong is your faith? Christian overcomes the obstacle only with the help of a fellow traveler named Hopeful. The key to belief, Hopeful explains, lies in the biblical passage, "He who comes to me I shall in no way cast out."[53] Now willing to put complete trust in God, Christian is able to cross the river and reach the Celestial City. Just as faith saved Bunyan himself in *Grace Abounding*, it saves Christian in *The Pilgrim's Progress*. Christian must call to mind God's goodness, and "live upon Him"[54] in his distress.

Bunyan made a daring choice when he decided to frame his tale as an allegory. Of all Protestant sects, the Puritans were the strictest biblical literalists. As noted by historian G. B. Harrison, their creed was "based on the Bible, and nothing but the Bible."[55] Puritans were thus strongly critical of the use of religious metaphor. The use of any metaphor, they believed, could open the door to a dangerously loose interpretation of scripture. Yet Bunyan took the risk of writing his greatest work "in the similitude of a dream." Why?

A recently published analysis suggests a persuasive answer. In *Literal Figures*, Thomas Luxon insightfully observes that living one's life in the radical trust demanded by Bunyan requires that a person live in a world where the unseen is more real than the seen.[56] In *The Pilgrim's Progress*, the man called Evangelist explains this in clear terms: "Believe steadfastly in things that are invisible. Let nothing that is on this side of the other world get within you."[57] The message of the book, therefore, is in agreement with the genre. In a sense, if they are to be saved, all Christians must walk through this world "in the similitude of a dream."

The strategy worked marvelously. The genius of *The Pilgrim's Progress*, notes Bunyan biographer Ola Winslow, was that it "translated a complex system of theology into a way of life simple enough to be understood by the least taught of those who listened."[58] G. B. Harrison adds, "The surprising fact is that Bunyan, who had hitherto written as the zealous teacher of a narrow puritan sect, should now produce a book which has been accepted into the shelves of many Christian sects in a vast number of languages."[59]

From a clinical viewpoint, *The Pilgrim's Progress*, like *Grace Abounding,* can be viewed as an obsessional struggle that is cured, in the end, through the finding of a new set of assumptions on which to direct one's life. Virtually the whole plot of Bunyan's momentous work consists of occasions when Christian falls away from his faith. When he corrects his thinking, he is saved. It is trust in God that saved Christian, just as it saved Bunyan, and it saved Luther before him.

Saint Thérèse

The Obsessions of the Little Flower

Autumn of 1883 was an extraordinarily difficult time for nine-year-old Thérèse Martin of Lisieux, France. Her schooling heretofore had been by home tutors. Now she was starting at a Catholic school for girls, enrolled with students from social and economic backgrounds vastly different from her own. Sensitive and shy by nature, she was unprepared for the social adjustment that would be required. To make matters worse, her excellence in reading had placed her with girls three to six years her elder. Little Thérèse was teased unmercifully for her airs of refinement (a teacher later remembered Thérèse as "the coddled child with the fancy ringlets"[1]), her goody-goody nature ("she never did anything wrong . . . a lot of the girls didn't like her because of that"), and her intelligence ("she usually took the prizes for the students").[2]

One student, in particular, was unrelenting. "She made me pay in a thousand ways for my little successes," Thérèse later recalled. "I didn't know how to defend myself and was content to cry without saying a word. The five years I spent in school were the saddest of my life."[3] The support of her sister Céline, her classmate and a year older, was critical. "If I hadn't had Céline with me, I couldn't have remained."

During the same year, another sister of Thérèse's, Pauline— twelve years her elder, her tutor while schooled at home, and her "second mother" after her mother's death when she was four—suddenly decided to enter a Carmelite convent. It was "as if a sword were buried in my heart," Thérèse would recall.[4] By Christmas, Thérèse was sleeping poorly and beset with constant headaches. Prayers were sought from priests and the extended family. Pauline wrote from the convent assuring Thérèse that she was "dreaming at night about the pains" in Thérèse's head and heart.[5]

On Easter Sunday of her tenth year, Thérèse abruptly began to feel ill. "I was seized with a strange trembling," Thérèse recounts. Immediately, she was put to bed. "Believing I was cold, my aunt covered me with blankets and surrounded me with hot water bottles. But nothing was able to stop my shaking which lasted almost all night."[6]

The disorder escalated rapidly. Over subsequent weeks, the child was struck by a panoply of severe neurological and psychiatric symptoms that continued a full six weeks. She waxed in and out of consciousness, she cried out in fear, at times she even suffered hallucinations and seizures. Thérèse's father lamented, "My little girl is either going crazy or is about to die." It was the most extraordinary illness. Thérèse herself called it "a forced and inexplicable struggle."[7] Everyone in the family attributed the illness to the work of the devil: It was his revenge on the Martin family for Pauline's having entered a convent. Then one day, after about six weeks, the terrifying malady rather suddenly abated. After a few minor relapses, Thérèse was free of its disabling symptoms. This episode is referred to as the "strange illness" of Saint Thérèse of Lisieux.

The Martyrdom of Simple Thoughts

Immediately on the heels of her strange illness, little Thérèse was struck by a barrage of tormenting thoughts. She had reported to her family that on the day she was cured of her strange illness, she had beheld a beautiful smile on the face of a statue of the Virgin Mary. Her family had concluded that Thérèse's cure was secondary to Mary's intervention. Pressed for details, however, Thérèse found that she could remember little about the experience. She was attacked by doubts. "I thought I had lied," she writes in her spiritual autobiography, *Story of a Soul*. "I was unable to look upon myself without a feeling of profound horror."[8]

Soon another agonizing worry struck: "I believed I had become ill on purpose." Thérèse desperately sought reassurance from others. "My confessor tried to calm me, saying it was not possible to pretend illness to the extent that I had been ill . . . [my sister] with her usual kindness reassured me." Even so, guilty thoughts continued to torment the troubled girl for almost a year.[9]

Subsequently, at age twelve, Thérèse experienced an onslaught of intrusive, agonizing worries more severe than any that she had experienced before. These were apparently triggered during her first religious retreat, by a priest's sermon on the subject of God's wrath. She became panic-stricken. As noted by Patricia O'Connor, one her best biographers, Thérèse became "paralyzed emotionally . . . by the fear that common thoughts were mortally sinful."[10] She lived in terror of offending God. "All my most simple thoughts and actions became the cause of trouble for me," Thérèse writes. "One would have to pass through this martyrdom to understand it well, and for me to express what I suffered would be impossible."[11]

One of her sisters recounts, "Thérèse went through a year and a half of terrible scruples about every detail of her behavior."[12] She sought constant reassurance from family members, particularly from her older sister Marie, on the state of her soul. "I had relief only when I told [my scruples] to Marie," Thérèse remembers.

> This cost me dearly, for I believed I was obliged to tell her the absurd thoughts I had even about her. As soon as I laid down my burden, I experienced peace for an instant; but this peace passed away like a lightning flash, and soon my martyrdom began over again. What patience my dear Marie needed to listen to me without showing any annoyance![13]

Marie was very insightful. She recognized that her sister suffered from scrupulosity, and employed a form of behavior therapy, decades before such a treatment was even considered by professionals. "Thérèse came to tell me all her so-called sins," Marie recounts. "I tried to cure her by allowing her to confess only two or three of them."[14] Marie also advised her sister not to burden her priest-confessor with her problems. As a result, Thérèse remembers,

> I told my scruples only to Marie, and was so obedient that my confessor never knew my ugly malady. I told him just the number of sins Marie permitted me to confess, not one more, and could pass as being the least scrupulous soul on earth in spite of the fact that I was scrupulous to the highest degree.[15]

Without a doubt, Thérèse suffered from a case of childhood obsessive-compulsive disorder. Thérèse suffered from classic, clinical obsessions: intrusive, repetitive, unwanted ideas that she herself recognized as "absurd." They caused her such torment that they drove her compulsively to seek support from others. As is true of all compulsions, the peace that reassurances provided did not last—in Thérèse's case, no longer than "a lightning flash."

Reassurance compulsions such as Thérèse describes are especially common in adolescent girls suffering obsessions of a religious, violent, or sexual nature. One of my patients, for instance, awoke at age twelve from a sound sleep with the thought of grabbing a knife and stabbing her parents. The overwhelming fear and guilt she felt prompted daily torrents of tearful requests for her parents' reassurance that she was not going to hurt them.

From a psychiatric perspective, Thérèse's hiding of her obsessive thoughts from her priest, as recommended by her sister, represented a form of "avoidance," a common secondary symptom of obsessive-compulsive disorder. She shied away from an activity in which she normally would have participated, because of her fear of her obsessions.

Obsessive-compulsive disorder is considered severe when it causes major interference in a person's life. This episode fits that criterion. Thérèse's father was forced to withdraw her from school at age thirteen because of constant anxiety and headaches. Once again, she was tutored at home. There, her obsessions continued to cause problems. She became, as adolescents with this disorder often do, overly sensitive and difficult. "I was really unbearable," Thérèse remembers, "because of my extreme touchiness."[16] One biographer describes Thérèse at this stage as "a fragile little queen."[17]

The Order of Carmelites Discalced

When Thérèse reached age fourteen, her obsessions and compulsions began to release their strong hold. She then entered a bright period and began developing plans to become a nun and live with her sister at Carmel.

Joining Carmel would prove no easy matter. For one thing, Thérèse was considered too young. In addition, her sister Marie had already joined Pauline in the convent, and Carmelite tradition prohibited more than two natural sisters from residing together in the same community. In spite of her reservations, however, the mother superior saw something special in Thérèse and relented. Thérèse was received as a member of the Carmelite order at age fifteen and was given a new, official name. In the context of this book it is arresting, indeed: "Sister Thérèse of the Child Jesus, OCD." The letters officially stand for "Order of Carmelites Discalced."

Life in the convent was almost unimaginably strict. The Discalced Carmelites were then, and still are, the most demanding of all Catholic orders for women. The nuns arose promptly at five o'clock a.m. to begin a thoroughly structured day including a lengthy mass, four hour-long periods of chanted prayers, five hours of work, and another one to two hours of private prayer. Silence was maintained constantly except during a brief recreation period.

Everything possible was done to assure an inward mental focus. The rule of "custody of the eyes," for instance, held that a nun should direct her eyes always at the ground. The nuns were totally cloistered, never leaving the convent for any reason; when they received guests, they talked through a barred grill.

To learn humility, a novice might be obliged to stand in the center of the common dining area, arms outstretched, and hear her faults enumerated. Penances included self-flagellation and the wearing of abrasive clothing or spiked religious medals. The goal was a constant recognition of sinfulness that would lead to a fervent desire for forgiveness. This "purgative way" had to be fully embraced before a nun could move on to the "illuminative" way, and finally to the mystical, or "unitive" state. Such was the spiritual path outlined by Theresa of Avila, the sixteenth-century ascetic genius who founded the order.

Over the centuries, the cloistered life has provided a meaningful framework for the spiritual development of countless women. For obsessive-compulsive disorder sufferers, in particular, the intensely regulated life in such settings can furnish much-needed structure and stability. The noted expert Pierre Janet, in fact, observed that individuals with OCD often do especially well in convents.[18] But the Carmel convent's extreme emphasis on personal sinfulness, shaped by the forbidding theology of nineteenth-century France, appears to have fed Thérèse's obsessions. She later observed, discreetly, that the Carmelite life "tends to too much self-reflection."[19]

In the convent she experienced emotional highs and lows. At times, she felt "extraordinary impulses of love." For a week as a novice she reports being "transported to heaven. . . . It was as if a veil had been thrown up between me and everything around me . . . I was no longer on earth; I did my work in the refectory as if someone had lent me a body."[20] At age sixteen she made peace with the "interior martyrdom" she had shouldered since age ten, the obsession that she had feigned her "strange illness." The catalyst was a compassionate priest who, as her confessor, asked Thérèse to consider a God who was forgiving, and who would never abandon her. She remembers this intervention as "the most consoling words I ever heard in my life . . . gratitude flooded my soul."[21]

At other times during these formative years she was attacked by new obsessional fears and doubts. One was the thought that she was misleading her superiors on the state of her soul, an obsession that drove her, once again, to inappropriate requests for reassurance. "I made the mistress come out of the choir," Thérèse recounts of one such incident, "and, filled with confusion, I told her the state of my soul. Fortunately, she saw things much clearer than I did, and she completely reassured me . . . nevertheless . . . I still wished to confide my strange temptation to our Mother Prioress, who simply laughed at me."[22]

Sexual obsessions were also a problem. A cousin who may well have suffered from obsessive-compulsive disorder herself and would later join Carmel, was tormented by thoughts of "nudity" while vacationing in Paris. Thérèse wrote back, "I understand everything, everything, everything! I know what these kinds of temptations are so well that I can assure you of this without any fear."[23]

Thérèse sums up the spiritual anguish of this period in her autobiography: "This was my way for five years: exteriorly nothing revealed my suffering which was all the more painful since I alone was aware of it."[24]

A Stratagem of Love

During these troubled years, Thérèse searched intensely for a religious perspective that would lessen her fears. She tried severe mortifications, night and day wearing a sharp-pointed scapular that cut deeply into her breast. But this only caused a troublesome infection, and a sense of increasing desolation. She concluded that such "astounding works" were forbidden to her, and never again performed severe penances.

She approached spiritual directors. Although she received some good advice at times, on the whole these directors were unhelpful, and several made her problems worse. One priest told her, "I forbid you in the name of God to call into question your being in the state of grace. . . . Banish, then, your worries. God wills it, and I command it!"[25] Another suggested: "Don't dwell on these [thoughts], it's very dangerous!"[26] Such advice is similar to that which Bunyan received—it only makes obsessions stronger. Finally, at age eighteen, after a priest emphasizing the sufferings in store for the unsaved brought her to tears, Thérèse gave up on spiritual directors for good.

Thérèse determined to find her own approach to healing. She became fascinated with gospel figures who had worked out their own individual paths to God. "There are great saints who have won heaven by their works," she explained one day to her sister Céline, "but my favorite patrons are those who stole it—like the holy innocents and the good thief. I want to imitate these thieves and win Heaven by stratagem, a stratagem of love which will open its gates to me."[27]

In a calculated and deliberate manner, Thérèse sought a new way of perceiving God, a new set of assumptions from which to view her tormenting fears. She searched for a *strategy* that would alleviate her suffering. At age twenty-one, she found it. She called it her "Little Way," sometimes referred to as the "way of spiritual childhood." By emphasizing God's mercy, more infinite than a parent's for a child, she found salvation in her own weakness. "Sanctity," Thérèse explains to her sister, is "a disposition of heart which is confident to the point of audacity in the goodness of our Father."[28] Like the prodigal son, no matter what sins she might commit, she could safely return to the arms of a God who would never forsake her.

It can hardly be overemphasized how different this view is from the majority of the teaching that Thérèse had been exposed to. The French Catholic church of her time remained under the influence of a morally rigorous movement known as Jansenism. By relying entirely on God's forgiveness, Thérèse was returning to a fundamental precept in Christian thought; she made this reliance the entire theme of her spirituality and developed the idea in a unique manner.

Thérèse subsequently required no spiritual director but God himself, "who does not teach me to count my acts; he teaches me to do everything for love . . . in peace."[29] With her Little Way in hand, she was able to accept her fearfulness and timidity, doubts and scruples, obsessions and compulsions, as all part of her "littleness," which was, in turn, always loved by God. Thérèse even found the strength to laugh at obsessions: "I will have the right of doing stupid things up until my death if I am humble and if I remain little!"[30]

As a result of her new outlook, Thérèse's life changed dramatically. She wrote, produced, and acted in plays. She composed poems that were shared with other Carmelite communities. She assumed the post of "novice master," directing women much older than herself. Recognizing Thérèse's budding talents, the mother superior of her convent began grooming Thérèse to succeed her. "Tall and robust, childlike, hiding the wisdom and discernment of a fifty-year-old, she is always composed, and in perfect control of herself in everything," wrote the sub-prioress. "She knows how to make you weep with devotion or die with laughter at recreation."[31] "I have known many fervent Carmelites," her mother superior remarked, "but Sister Thérèse's state of soul was so different from what I have seen in others that they seem to have nothing in common."[32]

The Trial of Faith

What Thérèse might have accomplished! But on Holy Thursday in the spring of 1896, at age twenty-three, she became sick and vomited blood. Highly intuitive as always, the young nun perceived that she was mortally ill. For more than a year, fevers and chest pains had troubled her. Now, doctors would confirm, the diagnosis was advanced tuberculosis. Thérèse would live out the remaining year and a half of her life in increasing agony. Pain medications were withheld, because Carmelites believed that they would lessen the spiritual gain accomplished through suffering.

Thérèse's intense physical distress brought on a period of devastating desolation, which Catholic biographers have referred to as her "trial of faith."[33] "He permitted my soul to be invaded by the thickest darkness," she writes. She remarked to her sister, "All the saints whom I love so much, where are they hanging out? I am not pretending, it's very true that I don't see a thing. Everything has disappeared on me."[34]

Severe obsessions and compulsions returned with a vengeance. "The thought of heaven," she writes, "was no longer anything but the cause of struggle and torment."[35] Her last obsessions took the form, primarily, of "temptations against the faith," intrusive, repugnant questioning of her deepest beliefs. "If you only knew what frightful thoughts obsess me!" she explains.[36] "It seems to me that the darkness, borrowing the voice of sinners, says mockingly to me: 'Death will not give you what you hope for but a night of nothingness.' . . . I don't want to write any longer about it; I fear I might blaspheme; I fear even that I have already said too much."[37] There were also sudden, intrusive profane words, similar to what Bunyan experienced: urges so strong that she bit her lips to resist them.[38]

Thérèse's compulsions during this period appear to have consisted primarily of repetitive religious acts such as crossing herself, glancing at religious objects, and making short invocations. "I undergo [my doubts] under duress," Thérèse explained, "but while undergoing them I never cease making acts of faith."[39] After nights of tormenting obsessions, Thérèse exclaimed, "Ah, how many acts of faith I made!"[40] She said at one point, "I believe I have made more acts of faith in the past year than I have in my whole life."[41]

The Little Way, as she had once conceived it, no longer seemed to provide consolation. Once again, Thérèse set her will on finding a strategy that would beat back this final trial. What was necessary, she realized, was an abandonment to God even more complete than ever before. "What would I become, if I were to rely upon my own strength?" she asked. "My temptations would become more violent and I would certainly succumb to them."[42] Unable to even so much as conjure up a positive image of God, she risked all on a faith supported by nothing she could either see or feel. She threw herself completely on "the blind hope that I have in God's mercy."[43]

Catholic theologians conclude that in doing so, Thérèse finally reached the Carmelite's ultimate goal, "mystical union with Christ." Thérèse herself concurs, marking the cost:

This saying of Job: "Although he should kill me, I will trust in him," has fascinated me from my childhood. But it took me a long time before I was established in this degree of abandonment. Now I am there; God has placed me there.[44]

101

With her strategy of total abandonment, Thérèse had again found a way to cast her tormenting thoughts in a new light. What about her doubts and blasphemies? "I don't dwell on them!" Thérèse told her sister. At the end of her life, even while suffering the most severe pain and darkness, she was able to report that "the ugly serpents are no longer hissing in my ears."[45] In the throes of death, she was, she insisted, interiorly at peace. A winsome smile is captured on her death mask.

Thérèse's Biographers

All of Thérèse's major biographers have recognized that she suffered from tormenting fears and doubts.[46] A number of them, however, have relied on outdated psychoanalytic theories to explain her unusual anxieties. Ida Görres, for instance, in the most complete psychological study of Thérèse yet undertaken, suggests that Thérèse suffered "an uncanny battle in the unconscious depths of her soul," "an eruption of overwhelming anxiety fantasies" from her youth.[47] Two of the most popular biographers of Thérèse, Patricia O'Connor and Monica Furlong, both suggest that she suffered a severe hysterical disorder caused by the awakening of hidden memories of her early years. One Catholic priest, in a recent work, has referred to Thérèse's problems as a "neurotic attack" and "conversion disorder."[48] The key assumption made by all these biographers is that Thérèse suffered severe psychological trauma in her early childhood, most likely linked to the loss of her mother to cancer at age four-and-a-half. By age five, according to this theory, Thérèse had developed a "dangerous" and "abnormal" state, characterized by "a morbid excess of conscientiousness."

These claims, however, stand in direct conflict to Thérèse's own accounts. Thérèse's entire theology rests on the loving recollections of her early years. Her spiritual path is nothing less than the "Way of Spiritual Childhood."[49] The claims, furthermore, can present a quandary for people drawn to follow the Little Way: Is her spiritual path based on neurotic denial? Such claims, in fact, could appear to bring the entire legacy of Saint Thérèse into question. It is therefore important to take a moment to examine them.

One unusual aspect of Thérèse's life is the immensity of detail that is known about it. In her autobiography, and also in 266 saved letters, Thérèse openly shares the minutiae of her most private worries, joys, victories and defeats, from toddler to adulthood, with a prodigious memory for detail. Her mother, sisters, and a cousin also wrote volumes of letters, and their favorite subject was the emotional, pious, strong-willed Thérèse. The majority of their letters were also carefully saved, providing a wealth of corroborating detail regarding the psychological climate of Thérèse's childhood.

The essential facts are as follows. Thérèse was born "very strong and healthy" into a well-to-do French family in 1873. Her parents, Louis and Zélie Martin, were both fervent Catholics. Indeed, both had once prepared to enter religious orders. Zélie was a nervous, extremely capable woman, who made her family wealthy by founding a lace-making business. Louis, reserved, perfectionist, and kindhearted to a fault, retired before the birth of Thérèse from a watchmaking career that had suited his temperament well, to a life

style that fitted him even better: long hours of daily prayer and exorbitant doting on his wife and daughters. His extraordinary devotion to Thérèse, his favorite, no doubt played some role in molding her lifelong trust in God's goodness.

Three older sisters also played large roles in Thérèse's life. All were extremely capable and bright. Each eventually joined Carmel. Céline, the closest to Thérèse in age, was a fine painter and photographer, and the saint's lifelong confidante. Marie helped Thérèse overcome her early scruples and later suggested that she write her autobiography. Pauline, a truly remarkable woman, reared Thérèse after Zélie died, first encouraged Thérèse to join Carmel, became mother superior in the convent, recognized before anyone else Thérèse's greatness, and saw to the posthumous publishing of the saint's works.

The household in which Thérèse was raised was exceptionally religious even for those times; and to a modern mind it was astonishingly so. A priest who frequented the Martin house observed that it resembled a convent. Each day started with mass at 6 a.m. Regular prayers were said at appointed hours. Sundays, feasts, and fasts were the major family events. Dinner conversation dwelt almost exclusively on spiritual topics and Catholic political concerns. The children were tutored in the catechism of the church before they learned to read. Thérèse may have been scarcely exaggerating when she wrote, "I was born in a holy soil, and impregnated with a virginal perfume.[50]

Yet, unlike the nuns at the convent that Thérèse later joined, the family members strongly expressed their affection. Thérèse, the youngest, was "devoured by kisses," cherished, pampered, and spoiled to an extraordinary degree. She never made her bed or combed her own hair until age eleven. "I was a child," Thérèse remarks, "who was fondled and cared for like few other children on earth."[51]

The child Thérèse was a joy to her whole family. She is described by her mother as "always very sweet," "very affectionate," "a little angel," and as "having "a heart of gold."[52] She is "an exceedingly thoughtful child," her mother wrote, "very honest . . . she wouldn't tell a lie for all the gold in the world."[53] Family members noted her unusual love for solitude. She would be "carried away" gazing at the stars, "just thinking."[54] And they noted her sensitivity. On one occasion, she was shown a picture of a skeleton and was "not able to endure this image."[55] Marie attempted to cure her little sister's fear of the dark by sending her to fetch things from dark rooms until she could do so without becoming frightened.

One imagines Thérèse as a lovable, dreamy, somewhat nervous girl who was truly happy and fulfilled in her role as the "little queen" of the Martin family. What about the "dangerous, abnormal emotional disturbance" that is hypothesized by some of her biographers? In examining Thérèse's childhood years one finds neither any unusual trauma or abuse nor any pathological signs such as withdrawal, depression, or inability to socialize.

There were only two childhood events that might reasonably be considered as having potential to cause long-lasting problems. At age three months, the baby Thérèse, because of fears that she was becoming malnourished, was given to a wet nurse, with whom she remained for almost a year, fully regaining her health. "The trauma of separation," biographer Furlong writes, fueled "the psychological pain suffered later."[56] Every letter written about Thérèse at this age, however, contradicts Furlong's assertion. The baby is repeatedly described as doing exceptionally well. Indeed, this wet nurse had splendidly nursed two of Zélie's previous babies.

The second time of stress, occurring at age four, is more important. "After the death of her mother," Görres concludes, Thérèse became "one of those oversensitive children for whom life itself represents an overwhelming burden." Thérèse herself writes of her terrible sadness at her mother's death. "My gaiety all went after Mother died," she remembers in her autobiography. "I had been so lively and open; now I became diffident and oversensitive, crying if anyone looked at me."[57]

But was Thérèse's reaction to her mother's death pathological? Soon after, Thérèse found new sources of loving support when the Martins joined their extended family in Lisieux. Every letter written about Thérèse from ages five to eight describes her as doing very well. Thérèse's aunt, with whom she spent much time, writes early on that "Thérèse seems to be very much at home," and later, that Thérèse is always "very happy."[58] Thérèse played with her sisters and cousin, participated actively in church, and did exceptionally well in her studies. Family members wrote no letters that expressed concern for Thérèse's psychological state. (In contrast, many letters were written expressing concern for the fourth of Thérèse's sisters, Léonie.) Thérèse herself says of these years, "My life passed by tranquilly and happily."[59]

There is no evidence of pathology. On the contrary, Thérèse appears to have enjoyed an abundance of love, encouragement, and stability. When she refers to her childhood as "the sunny years . . . stamped with smiles and the most tender caresses," we have no reason to think that neurotic denial poisons her recollections. When she sighs, "what a sweet imprint they have left on my soul," we have no reason to doubt what she says.[60]

The actual precipitating causes of Thérèse's severe case of childhood obsessive-compulsive disorder relate both to her family and school stresses and, particularly, to the long-term psychiatric manifestations of her "strange illness." These will be discussed in the next chapter.

The Greatest Saint of Modern Times

Today, Thérèse, the "Little Flower," is regarded by many as the most popular of all the Catholic saints after the Virgin Mary. She is the patroness of Russia, Mexico, and France. Her picture is seen on leaflets in most every Catholic church, adorns the classrooms of schools, and is featured on medals worn by countless admirers. Thérèse is the namesake of more than 1,700 churches, as well as perhaps the twentieth century's most famous Catholic, Mother Teresa of Calcutta. Thomas Merton entered the monastery after reading her works.

All this acclaim has befallen a quiet, cloistered nun who was completely unknown during her lifetime. Behind the walls of her convent, however, during a peak creative period that lasted from her late teens until her early death at twenty-four, Thérèse was a prodigious writer, composing poems, plays, an autobiography, and hundreds of letters. Her spiritual autobiography, *Story of a Soul,* became immensely popular shortly after her death. Within seven years it had been translated into nine languages, and within twenty, more than a million copies had been sold. It continues to be a Catholic best seller.

Part of the success of *Story of a Soul* is due to Thérèse's skill as a writer. Like John Bunyan, who also dropped out of school before age fifteen, Thérèse possessed astounding natural literary genius. Writing in a breathless, melodramatic style, she makes the austere life of a Carmelite nun exciting, touching, and even humorous to the modern reader—no small task. Her autobiography reads something like a romantic novel. Even her detractors admit that *Story of a Soul* is a literary tour de force.

Aside from writing ability, it is Thérèse's unique, down-to-earth spirituality that has carried her to fame. She seems more accessible, more real and modern, than other saints of the Catholic church. She talks of the significance of the latest scientific discoveries, of sexual temptations, and of obtaining medical care for her aging father. In her autobiography and other writings, she presents a simple strategy for reaching heaven, one that can be understood, if not followed, by any person, no matter how theologically unsophisticated. The Little Way, which she describes as "the way of trust and absolute surrender," is not a deep, difficult mysticism like that developed by her own namesake, Saint Theresa of Avila.

Thérèse's ideas, more than those of any other person, shaped the development of Catholic doctrine in the twentieth century. As noted by Pope John Paul II, "Thérèse [revealed] to the men and women of our day the fundamental reality of the Gospel." Pope Pius X called Thérèse the "greatest of modern-day saints"; Pius XI referred to her as "the star of my pontificate." In 1997, Thérèse was declared "Doctor of the

Universal Church" for her distinctive contribution to Catholic scholarship, a title accorded to only thirty-three people in history, and to only two other women. Her contribution, as that of both Bunyan and Luther, has been to move Christian theology closer to a position of fundamental trust in God's mercy.

What Causes Obsessive-Compulsive Disorder?

Obsessive-compulsive disorder was once regarded as the most obscure and puzzling of all mental disorders. The crux of the problem is this: its sufferers tend to be intelligent, reasonable, and successful individuals; therefore, how can they allow themselves to be upended by thoughts that they know are senseless? And why can't they stop performing their silly rituals?

Sir Aubrey Lewis, the great British psychiatrist, observed in 1935 the apparent contradictions in obsessive-compulsive disorder "between kindness and cruelty, logicality and unreason, fear and desire." After pointing out OCD's overwhelming "variety of problems and the difficulty of stating them," he concluded: "It may well be that obsessional illness cannot be understood without understanding the nature of man."[1]

Over the last two decades, however, by virtue of an unprecedented international research effort—one that has produced more than a thousand scientific articles each year—the cause of obsessions and compulsions has finally been revealed. It is now clear that the disorder arises out of a combination of specific psychological, cultural, and biological factors.

This chapter begins with a critique of the Freudian theory of obsessive-compulsive disorder, now widely discredited but still widely influential. It then summarizes a large number of recent psychological studies that provide a commonsense explanation for OCD's baffling symptoms. Finally, the chapter touches on recent epidemiological and biochemical studies that complete our understanding of this disorder and make clear the genesis of the tormenting thoughts that afflicted Luther, Bunyan, and Thérèse.

Freudian Theory

Sigmund Freud, the twentieth century's most famous psychiatrist, was fascinated by obsessive-compulsive disorder. He published fourteen major papers on it, more than on any other topic. Freud believed that the puzzle of OCD could be well explained by his psychoanalytic theories, that obsessive thoughts, in fact, represented a perfect model for the psychological conflicts he hypothesized were raging in his patients' minds.

The great psychoanalyst speculated that obsessive-compulsive disorder began in childhood, when a boy or girl instinctively wanted to behave in a sexual or aggressive manner but was prevented by a parent from doing so. The ensuing parent-child conflict, if not satisfactorily resolved, resulted in "repression" of the conflict into the unconscious. This conflict, needing to be discharged, was released later in life in transmuted forms through the development of obsessions and compulsions.

In 1909 Freud illustrated his theory in a captivating case study, "Notes upon a Case of Obsessional Neurosis." It involves "a youngish man of university education" who had become virtually incapacitated by blasphemous religious thoughts, repugnant sexual ideas, and terrifying images of rats eating his intestines. Freud hypothesized that this patient developed these obsessions because he had repressed into his unconscious his "infantile hatred of his father." After psychoanalysis, Freud reported, his patient became aware of the conflicts that fueled his obsessions and compulsions, and was able to resolve them.

Psychoanalysis dominated American psychiatry for much of the twentieth century. As a medical student training in psychiatry in the early 1970s, I was encouraged to delve into my obsessional patients' childhoods and to search for unconscious conflicts. Since then, much of Freud's theory has fallen out of favor. Still, the major thrust of his formulation lingers on in the idea that obsessional thoughts reflect unconscious urges and desires that are genuine.

According to our modern scientific understanding of obsessive-compulsive disorder, however, just the opposite is true. In the current view, obsessions are fleeting, irrational thoughts that have no base at all in genuine desire. Extensive research has been unable to establish any connection between obsessions and conflicts carried from childhood. Studies show, on the contrary, that OCD sufferers tend to come from families that are relatively stable and free of conflict. In addition, psychotherapies that target unconscious conflicts, such as psychoanalysis, have proven ineffective in the treatment of obsessions and compulsions.[2]

The importance of these findings cannot be overstated. Consider a typical case. A young mother is struck by the obsessional thought of grabbing a knife and harming her baby. One of my patients, struck by such a thought, called 911 and insisted on being locked up in our community hospital psychiatric unit. Another patient revealed a similar obsession to a friend and the next day found a social worker at her doorstep. Does a woman with this obsession really, in some deep recess of her mind, want to harm her child?

Experts in the field of obsessive-compulsive disorder are now in unanimous agreement that obsessional thoughts never represent genuine desires or urges. The most enlightening work in this area has come from investigators in the field of cognitive psychology, the study of how we think. According to this research, the cause of obsessive-compulsive disorder may be summed up in four steps.

An Up-to-Date Psychological Model for the Cause of Obsessive-Compulsive Disorder

Step #1. *A "normal" anxiety-producing thought enters the mind.* It can't be overemphasized that the thoughts that become tormenting in obsessive-compulsive disorder are not, in themselves, pathological or indicative of mental disorder. Rather, they are a normal part of human experience.

Psychologist Stanley Rachman of the University of British Columbia, considered by many the world's leading expert on this disorder, first clarified the commonplace nature of obsessions in a landmark paper published in 1978.[3] Rachman asked 124 students, hospital workers, and nurses: "Do you ever get thoughts or impulses that are intrusive and unacceptable?" Fully 80 percent answered yes, they had such thoughts at least once a week. Dr. Rachman and his coworkers then transcribed these "unacceptable thoughts" and placed them alongside the obsessions of OCD patients. The experts could not tell the difference between the unacceptable thoughts of average people and the obsessions of individuals afflicted with the disorder.

The plain fact is this: most people routinely experience thoughts that are exactly the same in content as clinical obsessions. This fact has now been verified by over a dozen studies. For instance, a 1992 study details the percentages of all people who report various types of unacceptable thoughts. Here are a few of them: 55 percent of adults have impulses to crash their cars; 42 percent have urges to jump from high places; 25 percent experience thoughts that their phones are contaminated;

112

13 percent have images of exposing themselves in public; and a full 13 percent have thoughts to fatally stab loved ones. The only difference between these people and the sufferers of obsessive-compulsive disorder is that the latter experience obsessions more often and feel them more strongly.[4]

Step #2. *The anxiety-producing thought is evaluated abnormally.* Here is where the problems begin. In the 1960s and 1970s researchers at the University of Pennsylvania, led by psychiatrist Aaron Beck, demonstrated that we all possess an automatic, almost instantaneous, evaluative process that lies outside our conscious awareness. Its function is to assign different levels of importance, or attentional value, to the ideas, images, and urges that come into our minds. In the 1980s, cognitive psychologists applied Beck's findings to the development of obsessions. They discovered that the critical moment in the development of obsessive-compulsive disorder occurs when a person assigns a fearful thought a special importance. As Rachman puts it, "The majority of people dismiss or ignore their unwanted thoughts and regard them as dross. However, once a person attaches important meaning to these unwanted thoughts, they tend to become distressing and adhesive."[5]

The average person, struck by an unwanted idea, image, or urge, says to herself something like, "What a dumb thought!" Then she shakes her head and turns her mind to another subject, and the thought disappears. If that person has obsessive-compulsive disorder, however, the thought stays in her mind. What happens is that the intrusive thought provokes a kind of false alarm ("Something is wrong, and I must do something about it!"). Instead of being dismissed from consciousness as it should, it is given an inappropriate significance that propels it into the spotlight of attention.

Step #3. *The sufferer fights to get the thought out of mind.* Recognizing the irrationality or inappropriateness of the thought that has taken over her awareness, the OCD sufferer naturally attempts to push it out of her mind. The mind, however, does not work like a computer, where a string of words can simply be backspaced or deleted. Rather, it is as if the mind says, "Because you have worked so hard to get rid of this thought, it must be very important. Therefore, I will make sure to bring it back to consciousness again!"

The frustrating outcome of "thought suppression" was first demonstrated experimentally by psychologist Daniel Wegner in 1987 at Trinity University in San Antonio, Texas. In a famous investigation, Wegner divided his subjects into two groups. One group was told a short story about white bears, while the other was told not to think about such animals. As you might guess, the group told not to think about white bears had bear-thoughts throughout the day, while the other group rapidly forgot about them. The conclusion: Trying not to think a thought only makes it come back stronger. OCD sufferers unwittingly turn normal unwanted thoughts into agonizing obsessions by resisting them and trying to force them out of conscious awareness.[6]

Step #4. *The sufferer performs specific acts over and over in order to allay the anxiety caused by obsessions.* A large number of research studies have demonstrated that although such acts, compulsions, do provide short-term relief, in the long run they only make obsessions stronger. OCD sufferers realize that their compulsive acts are self-defeating, yet they can't stop themselves from repeating them.

One part of the problem is the surprising power of "negative reinforcement," the automatic tendency to repeat any act that seems like it might have prevented a feared outcome. An individual will be drawn to check the stove again, for instance, simply because the last time he did it a fire did not start. Negative reinforcement, however, does not fully explain all aspects of compulsive behavior. For instance, it can't account for why compulsions are so eerily stereotyped—performed exactly the same way time after time. Research by leading OCD expert Judith Rapoport and her team at the National Institutes of Health has shed light on this issue.

In a lecture titled "Hand-Washing People and Paw-Licking Dogs," Rapoport suggests that the stereotypy of compulsions is explained by their close relationship to "fixed action patterns," certain habits of behavior that are hardwired into the brains of all animals.[7] Cats lick their faces and paws in just the same manner many times a day. Male fiddler crabs perform elaborate movements, invariable in form and timing, with one of their two claws before mating. These and a myriad of other examples represent rituals of behavior performed quickly and automatically, having value for evolutionary survival.

These same fixed action patterns, however, are sometimes set off when they shouldn't be, especially in stressful situations. For instance, dogs under stress may start compulsively licking their paws, a sometimes injurious response that can lead to painful sores. In the case of humans, Rapoport and others have speculated that compulsive acts represent our own inappropriately discharged fixed action patterns.

The Special Role of Personal Responsibility

We have seen that the crucial step in the development of a clinical obsession is the assignment of undue importance to certain thoughts. In 1989 psychologist Paul Salkovskis of Oxford, England, proposed a theory to explain why this faulty evaluation occurs. The key, Salkovskis surmised, is that "intrusive thoughts are mistakenly interpreted as indicating that a person may be responsible for harm to self or others."[8] Obvious, right? Of course obsessive-compulsives check the stove because they feel responsible for preventing danger—why else would they do it? Yet Salkovskis's idea nicely explains a number of common clinical observations.

OCD sufferers, for instance, never obsess about purely chance events, such as being caught in an earthquake or a hurricane. Why? Because the obsessional patient plays no role in the occurrence or the prevention of such happenings. Obsessional individuals do, on the other hand, readily develop symptoms when thcy are put into situations where obvious harm may occur as a result of their actions. A striking example is the frequent onset of obsessions and compulsions in women after the birth of a first child. Approximately 20 percent of all females with obsessive-compulsive disorder suffer its onset (almost always related to the safety of their babies) at this time of unparalleled assumption of personal responsibility.

Another example: It has often been observed that people with obsessive-compulsive disorder experience a "holiday" from their disorder when they find themselves in a new environment—that is, until they become accustomed to the place. Once I admitted to the hospital a student who suffered from severe checking compulsions. He did fine for a few days; in fact, our staff wondered why I had admitted him at all. Then he started setting off fire alarms, ear-piercing whistles that sent our mental health unit into turmoil. Why did he begin compulsively setting off the alarms when he did? My patient later explained, apologetically, that obsessions dealing with harm happening to friends were a long-term problem. When he had arrived on the unit, however, he had felt calm because he didn't know anybody. In a few days, however, his feelings began to change. "I began to make friends," he told me, "and I felt responsible for their safety." It was then that he was driven by obsessions of fires to set off the alarms.

Several dozen well-designed experimental studies have lent strong support to Salkovskis's theory. A recent article in *Behavior Research and Therapy* summarizes the results of studies using psychological tests to compare OCD sufferers with other groups of people. Obsessionals, it is clear, have many more "inflated responsibility" beliefs than "normals," or than people

116

suffering from depression, panic disorder, generalized anxiety, or phobias. These beliefs include both general assumptions ("I am often close to causing harm") and specific interpretations of intrusive thoughts ("Since I've had this thought, I must want it to happen"). In no other mental disorder do people feel so accountable for danger.[9]

This inflated sense of personal responsibility has been demonstrated experimentally in a number of ways. One consistent finding is that when an obsessional person is alone, both anxiety and the tendency to perform compulsions increase. Roz Shafran of the University of British Columbia, for instance, asked a group of people with contamination obsessions to touch a toilet seat and then refrain from washing. They were to perform the task alone, then in the presence of an examiner. Shafran found that obsessive-compulsives experienced much less anxiety and fewer urges to perform compulsions when another person was present—that is, when they felt less individual responsibility for the outcome.[10]

In another study, psychologist Edna Foa of the University of Pennsylvania, a longtime leader in research in anxiety disorders, compared the responses of OCD sufferers, phobics, and a "normal" control group to differing levels of imagined danger: high risk ("You see that a person sitting alone in a diner is choking"), medium risk ("You see some nails on a road"), and no significant risk ("You see a piece of string on the ground"). In the last two situations, OCD patients felt more responsible for outcome, and experienced more anxiety and more urges to check that harm would not occur. Foa concluded that these findings indicate "strong support for the hypothesis that inflated responsibility is an important factor in obsessive-compulsive disorder."[11]

A related finding is that OCD sufferers appear to experience a unique information-processing error. Normally, people can readily distinguish between causing harm and failing to prevent it—a presumption that is extensively reflected in our legal code.

117

To hit a person with your car, for instance, is worse than failing to keep someone from being struck. Obsessionals, however, do not appear to make this distinction. For them, researchers at Oxford University have recently concluded, "failing to try to prevent harm to self or others is the same as having caused the harm in the first place."[12]

The personalities of obsessive-compulsive disorder suffer-ers—the deep, lifelong patterns of thinking and behavior that mark them as individuals—are recognized as reflecting an especially strong sense of personal responsibility. In Stanley Rachman's 1980 book, *Obsessions and Compulsions*, considered by some to be the most complete work on the disorder ever written, obsessionals are described as "correct, upright, moral citizens who aspire to high standards of personal conduct."[13] In earlier centuries, astute observers made similar observations. "They are mostly good people," wrote English Bishop John Moore in 1692, "for bad men rarely know anything of these types of thoughts."[14]

Culture and Obsessive-Compulsive Disorder

Rudolf Virchow, a renowned German sociologist of the nine-teenth century, was the first to observe that just as epidemics of infectious disease spring up with massive social and cultural changes (e.g., the Black Plague, brought to Europe as a result of burgeoning international trade in the Renaissance), so epidemics of mental illnesses can spring up in critical junctures of history that are characterized by political and intellectual revolution. Contemporary leaders in the field of mental health have tended to ignore this cultural dimension of mental illness. One exception, however, is Harvard's brilliant anthropologist Arthur Kleinman. In a series of convincing articles and books, Kleinman has demonstrated marked differences in the occurrences of various mood disorders, particularly depression, between

Eastern and Western societies. Other researchers have looked at cultural factors that affect the onset of schizophrenia and anorexia nervosa.

Obsessive-compulsive disorder has been largely overlooked in this regard, even though there is tantalizing evidence to suggest that the onset of the disorder is very much culture-related. As far as can be told, for instance, obsessive-compulsive disorder was never a major problem in any society prior to the Renaissance in Western Europe. Father Ladislas Orsy of Georgetown University, an expert in the field of moral theology, observes that scrupulosity was rarely mentioned in the first five or six centuries of Christian writings and became commonplace only in the Renaissance. Consistent with this view, J. Jerome, writing in the French review *La Vie Spirituelle,* offers the opinion that severe cases of scruples simply did not exist prior to the late Middle Ages.[15]

Salkovskis's insight into the role of personal responsibility in the development of obsessions makes clear why this is so. Prior to the teachings of the Fourth Lateran Council of 1215, Christians in Western Europe felt no burden of responsibility for pleasing God. As long as they were members of the church in good standing, they could rest in a reasonable belief that their eternal salvation was assured.

That Lateran Council, however, radically altered the personal responsibility that each Christian shouldered for salvation. As discussed in chapter 2, the fundamental assumption became that each Christian could know and weigh his own sins and could determine for himself his own eternal destiny. The ruling that each Christian had to regularly confess his sins, along with the soon-to-follow declaration that thoughts themselves could represent mortal sins, dramatically changed the lives of all who were prone to obsessions. It exponentially multiplied the role of personal responsibility. Suddenly, Renaissance Europe became a hothouse for the development of obsessive-compulsive disorder.

Personal responsibility increased in all areas of life as individualism and self-determination flourished. In this day, people shoulder a weight of personal responsibility for their well-being that was unheard-of a millennium ago. Thus, the epidemic of obsessive-compulsive disorder continues, even though in secular societies the main topics of obsessions have changed.

The Biochemistry of Obsessive-Compulsive Disorder

Obsessive-compulsive disorder is clearly a psychological disorder, manifested in a person's thoughts and aggravated by that person's attempts to suppress them. We have seen that it is also a cultural disorder. It is a biochemical, or medical, disorder as well.

Indeed, the majority of recent scientific papers on OCD deal with the biomedical aspect of the illness. Research in this area is so impressive that the United States Congress has seen fit to include OCD among a small group of mental disorders covered by the Mental Health Equitable Treatment Act. Thus, OCD has been officially recognized as being just as "biologically based" as diabetes or heart disease, and therefore deserving of the same insurance coverage.

The occurrence of obsessions and compulsions has been irrefutably linked to chemical changes in the brain. Studies of neurotransmitters—chemicals that serve as messengers between brain cells—reveal that one called serotonin is abnormally active in individuals who suffer from obsessive-compulsive disorder. When concentrations of this neurotransmitter are altered by medications, the severity of the disorder changes dramatically.

Studies of brain anatomy demonstrate that OCD sufferers possess a larger number of working brain cells than other people. This interesting finding makes intuitive sense, since their problem is that they think too much. As it turns out, all of us are born with an excess of brain cells. Their absolute numbers decrease through the years as our brains become more streamlined and efficient, a process referred to as "pruning." There is speculation that obsessive-compulsive disorder may reflect a failure in this aspect of brain maturation.

Studies of brain physiology provide the most dramatic evidence for obsessive-compulsive disorder's biochemical roots. Advanced brain-scanning techniques, such as positron emission tomography (PET) and magnetic resonance imaging (MRI), allow researchers to see where brain cells are actively at work. For instance, if a person is scanned while studying a book, the visual center in the back of the brain lights up on the screen. If a person is solving a puzzle, the frontal lobe stands out. In people suffering from obsessions, it is the basal ganglia, a grapelike cluster of cells located deep in the brain, that lights up abnormally. Aberrations in the basal ganglia are apparent in obsessional patients at rest, and they increase when patients are exposed to situations that intensify their obsessional fears.

It is now widely agreed that on a biochemical level, the cause of obsessive-compulsive disorder rests in the basal ganglia. Some experts now even refer to OCD as a "basal ganglia disease." Stroke, head injury, and carbon monoxide poisoning can all cause the occurrence of obsessions and compulsions when they damage the nerve cells of this region. Even streptococcal infections ("strep throat") can lead to obsessive-compulsive disorder through the production of antistreptococcal antibodies that damage the basal ganglia.

Overall, it appears that the most frequent cause of basal-ganglia abnormality is an inherited vulnerability. Studies indicate that if an individual has obsessive-compulsive disorder, then the chance that an immediate relative will also suffer the disorder is increased more than fourfold. Twin studies, which establish genetic cause with greater certainty, indicate that identical twins suffer from OCD almost twice as often as fraternal twins. These findings are considered to be decisive

121

proof of genetic cause. The consensus is that inherited factors account for 50 percent or more of OCD's occurrence.

Why would abnormalities in the basal ganglia cause obsessions? Two decades ago, all that was known for sure about the basal ganglia was that it coordinated involuntary movements, those body motions that are done without the need of our thinking about them, such as walking. Recent research shows, however, that the basal ganglia coordinates not only movements, but also our awareness of our thoughts.

Nobel Prize–winning researcher Gerald Edelman has done some of the key work in this area. In his recent book *A Universe of Consciousness,* written with Giulio Tononi, Edelman concludes that conscious awareness results from the electrical discharges of elaborate, ever-changing meshes of rapidly firing brain cells called "dynamic cores." While the basal ganglia does not contain these cores, Edelman posits, its cells are arranged in a manner that allows them to direct what goes into and comes out of them. In certain situations when the basal ganglia is defective, he notes, "obsessions are forced upon one's consciousness."[16]

Harvard's Roger Pitman suggests a helpful analogy: The basal ganglia works like a computer using a match-mismatch mechanism to identify certain thoughts that are of special importance for survival—specifically, those conveying a danger message. In the basal ganglia, an image or idea is compared against preexisting wishes, fears, and memory traces. If there is a match, the thought harmonizes with associations about the self and the world, and it is dismissed from consciousness. If there is not a match, the idea is returned to the cortical areas of the brain for further conscious appraisals. Normally, an idea is dismissed when it should be—when, through conscious reflection, an individual realizes that danger does not lurk. In obsessive-compulsive disorder, however, the idea is kept in strong conscious awareness long after the individual himself knows that it should be dismissed. Obsessional thoughts, according to Pitman, result from match-mismatch errors occurring in the basal ganglia.[17]

Another way to look at this, also purely speculative, is that humans have developed through evolution a unique brain-module located in the basal ganglia that regulates the flow of thoughts of personal responsibility into and out of conscious awareness. The apparatus "decides," on an automatic, almost instantaneous basis, whether a particular fearful idea, image, or urge should be dismissed from consciousness or kept there for further processing. Such a module would have survival value, since thoughts of personal responsibility deserve special consideration—surviving depends on recognizing and dealing with dangers that can be prevented, while, on the other hand, there is little point in dwelling on those that cannot. In obsessive-compulsive disorder, it is the "responsibility-module" that breaks down.

In summary, obsessive-compulsive disorder is, at once, a psychological, cultural, and biomedical condition. This is not unusual; a number of medical conditions share this same multiplicity of causes. High blood pressure, for instance, is directly related to psychological stress, and to a certain personality organization (the "type A," characterized by hostility, competitiveness, and time urgency). It is also very much a cultural disorder. Migrations from rural to urban settings have been repeatedly shown to result in outbreaks of its occurrence. In high blood pressure and OCD alike, the causes are hard to tease apart. One may stand out in a given case, but it is difficult to speak generally about which is more fundamental.

Luther, Bunyan, and Thérèse

In the cases of obsessive-compulsive disorder suffered by Luther, Bunyan, and Thérèse, psychological, cultural, and biochemical factors all played their roles. The obsessions of all three figures began as normal thoughts. Luther, for instance, was struck by the common enough concern that he hadn't confessed all his sins. What happened then, however, was something pathological: his mind gave the thought an extra salience that it shouldn't have received. He felt overly responsible for it, and it stuck in his mind when it should have been dismissed. A similar process occurred to Bunyan when he experienced his "sell Christ" thought, and to the adolescent Thérèse when she feared that she might have lied about her "strange illness." All three tried hard to stop thinking these thoughts and were caught in the "white bear trap": by attempting to push the thoughts away, they only guaranteed that the thoughts would come back even stronger. Finally, all three developed compulsive behaviors that were designed to put right the obsessions. Unfortunately, these, too, only had the effect of making their tormenting thoughts even stronger.

From a cultural perspective, Luther, Bunyan, and Thérèse were all caught up in the epidemic of religious obsessions that began in the early Renaissance. If they had lived in an earlier age when personal responsibility weighed less on the individual soul, they might not have developed obsessive-compulsive disorder.

Considering biochemical causes, it seems likely that Luther, Bunyan, and Thérèse were all to some extent genetically prone to develop obsessions and compulsions. Most OCD sufferers are. The fact that all three were especially sensitive and guilt-prone when young suggests an inherited predisposition to anxiety.

The Biochemical Roots of Thérèse's OCD

The case of Thérèse is especially interesting in this regard. It was in her hapless tenth year that she developed what her family referred to as her "strange illness," made manifest in an astonishing variety of neurological and psychiatric symptoms.

A maid recalls Thérèse being "seized by attacks of fright and hallucinations several times a day."[18] A sister remembers that "she used to stand up in bed, bend down and execute a kind of somersault which caused her to go flying over the end of the bed and land heavily on the floor."[19] A cousin reports "propulsive seizures during which she made wheel-like movements that she would have been absolutely incapable of making in a state of health."[20] Thérèse describes her unusual psychological state in *Story of a Soul*: "I was absolutely terrified of everything: my bed seemed to be surrounded by frightful precipices; making me cry out in fear. . . . I often appeared to be in a faint, not making the slightest movement, and yet I heard everything that was said around me."[21]

Family members were perplexed that Thérèse's agitated states could be triggered by their own reactions to her symptoms. "I used to play tricks," explained Marie, the sister who was primarily in charge of Thérèse at this time. "When I made believe that I had no fear whatsoever, then she would keep quiet; but if I were to show the least bit of fear, she would begin again with renewed vigor."[22]

Thérèse was treated by the Martins' family physician, Dr. Notta, who prescribed close observation, cool baths, and the application of moist compresses. The good doctor was initially perplexed as to the nature of the illness. In the end, however, he diagnosed it as a severe case of a disorder not uncommon in that day: Saint Vitus' dance.

Now more commonly known as Sydenham chorea, Saint Vitus' dance, according to a recent textbook, is characterized by "jerking movements of the arm and flinging movements of the legs. . . . The severity of involuntary movements is greatly influenced by emotional factors. The child is fretful, irritable, or emotionally unstable. In severe cases, mental confusion, agitation, hallucination, and delusions may occur."[23] The disorder typically strikes girls between the ages of five and fifteen, and runs a course of six to twelve weeks.

Sydenham chorea has recently been the subject of significant research. Studies have demonstrated it to be an autoimmune disease somewhat similar to rheumatic fever, in which wayward antibodies to streptococcal bacteria attack healthy heart cells. In Sydenham's, the same type of bacteria attack the brain's basal ganglia.

In the late 1980s, at the National Institutes of Mental Health, Susan Swedo and colleagues demonstrated that the occurrence of Sydenham's is directly associated with the onset of obsessive-compulsive disorder. In Swedo's studies, more than half the children with Sydenham's developed obsessions and compulsions; none of them had these symptoms prior to the onset of the illness. There are no other medical or neurological disorders that bear such an association with obsessive-compulsive disorder.[24]

Before her strange illness, Thérèse was a normal, if overly anxious, little girl. Afterward, much of her life was consumed by finding ways to deal with tormenting thoughts. It appears that a simple bacterial infection was the proximal cause of her obsessive-compulsive disorder.

It is also interesting to note studies suggesting that reoccurrences of strep throat may exacerbate OCD, especially since Thérèse was hampered by sore throats during both of her severe episodes of obsessive-compulsive disorder. As a child, "Little Therese was sick every winter . . . with colds and bronchitis."[25] At age eleven, while still suffering her first obsessive-compulsive disorder episode, she was "coughing very much."[26] Then she was free of both respiratory illnesses and severe obsessions and compulsions through most of her teenage years ("at Carmel she hardly ever had colds").[27] In her early twenties, however, just prior to the onset of her second major episode of obsessive-compulsive disorder, we find this report: "Sister Therese . . . is always having her bouts with sore throats."[28] It is possible that not only Thérèse's initial episode of obsessive-compulsive disorder, but also her frequent exacerbations of the disorder, were triggered by recurrent strep throat.

126

Thérèse and her family attributed her recovery from Saint Vitus' dance to a miracle, "the Virgin's smile." Yet the damage to her basal ganglia was not completely cured. It precipitated her severe obsessions and compulsions. If one were so inclined, one might conclude that God worked an even greater miracle than completely curing her: God used a lowly streptococcal infection to catalyze the theological triumphs of a sheltered and dreamy French girl who was a very unlikely candidate to become one of his very greatest saints.

Addressing the Stigma of OCD

Recently, I mentioned to a friend of mine, a Jesuit priest, that Ignatius of Loyola had most likely suffered from obsessive-compulsive disorder. My observation was met with stony silence. Then I told another friend (a devout Baptist who, I later learned, keeps Luther's *Table Talk* by his bedside) that Martin Luther had suffered from the disorder. This friend took it as personal affront. "You know, I really wouldn't like to think that," he said, a bit defiantly.

The sad fact is that even today to apply the label of OCD is often to call into question a person's broader mental abilities. This mistaken view is related to an assumption that was once widely held in psychiatry: that the brain functions as a unitary organ, same as the heart or liver; if one part is damaged, it inevitably affects the function of the organ as a whole. If this were true, then the fact that Luther had a mental disorder would indeed imply that his ability to think clearly about anything was at least somewhat impaired.

It is now obvious, however, that the brain is not a unified whole, but a collection of hundreds of unique modules. Rather than a single organ, it more closely resembles the entire body, with a large number of different and independently functioning parts. Just as an injured shoulder does not affect the lungs, an

127

inability to dismiss certain thoughts does not diminish a person's larger ability to reason both analytically and creatively.

The results of two decades of intensive research prove that obsessive-compulsive disorder is a specific and limited brain disorder. So when we say that people such as Luther and Ignatius suffered from obsessive-compulsive disorder, we are not impugning their greatness—no more than if we said they suffered from tics, or stuttering, or color-blindness.

7

Treating Obsessive-Compulsive Disorder

When I was in medical training in the 1970s, therapy for obsessive-compulsive disorder was next to worthless. If a patient had a severe case, my professors would just shake their heads. Now the situation is dramatically different. To the surprise of psychiatrists everywhere, OCD has been shown to be one of the most treatable of all mental disorders.

A group of medications referred to as "serotonin reuptake inhibitors" has been proven specifically effective by hundreds of studies from major academic centers. Two forms of psychological treatment, as well, have proven worthy: behavior therapy and cognitive therapy. Used individually or in combination, these treatments can markedly help 60 to 80 percent of OCD sufferers. None of them, unfortunately, completely cures a patient's obsessions and compulsions in the manner, say, that penicillin eradicates pneumonia. But with therapy, the power of tormenting thoughts can be drained away. People can be "cured" in the sense that their obsessions and compulsions are rendered manageable.

This chapter focuses on the two proven psychological treatments for obsessive-compulsive disorder. Behavioral therapy is the gold standard. With the single exception of the treatment of simple phobias, such as a fear of snakes, no psychotherapy for any type of mental disorder has been shown to be more effective. Cognitive therapy has been less studied but may work equally well. Usually, in practice, it is combined with behavior therapy to form "cognitive-behavioral therapy." In addition, a new procedure holding much promise is "responsibility modification therapy." A brief examination of this last approach will set the stage for understanding the cure that was found by Luther, Bunyan, and Thérèse.

Behavior Therapy for OCD

In 1969 the English psychologist Victor Meyer performed a landmark experiment. He hospitalized fifteen patients with severe obsessive-compulsive disorder. All were disabled by terrifying fears of germs and performed washing and cleaning rituals that took hours a day. All had failed to benefit from previous intensive treatments. Meyer employed a novel approach: he exposed the patients to their most feared contaminants and then prevented them from doing any cleaning or washing at all. One person would be directed to put dirt on her hands, for instance, and allow them to remain soiled for days at a time, enduring the terrible anxiety that ensued. After repeated exposure to their obsessional fears, and prevention from performing their cleaning compulsions, ten patients were much improved or symptom-free, and five were moderately improved. A follow-up study revealed that after five years only two patients had relapsed.[1]

Meyer employed a form of behavior therapy, a treatment first discovered by psychiatrist Joseph Wolpe of Temple University

130

and others in the 1950s as a cure for simple phobias. Suppose a man had an overwhelming fear of riding in elevators. Studies showed that he could completely overcome his fear by repeatedly exposing himself to them and preventing himself from escaping. If an individual made himself enter elevators a sufficient number of times (usually about thirty), and each time stayed long enough for his anxiety to diminish (as a rule, not longer than an hour), then eventually he overcame his fear of elevators.

The effectiveness of behavior therapy rests in the principle of habituation, a basic, physiological property of the nervous system found in all animals from mollusks to man. If a snail's head is lightly touched, it recoils quickly into its shell. If it is touched fifteen times in a row, however, it stops withdrawing. The snail, in effect, gets used to being touched: that's habituation. The same type of response occurs in the infinitely more complicated case of a human who is afraid of a certain situation. Like the snail, if a person is presented with a noxious stimulus repeatedly, and neither escapes from it nor is harmed by it, then he or she will eventually get used to it.

Behavior therapy is a commonsense sort of treatment. What it amounts to, in essence, is helping patients face up to their fears. Meyer's genius was in recognizing the similarity between obsessive-compulsive disorder and a simple phobia. He saw that both are triggered by particular fears: in a phobia, a fearful situation; in obsessive-compulsive disorder, a terrifying thought. Further, Meyer saw that both are made worse by repeated escape responses: in a phobia, the escape response is running away from the feared situation, while in obsessive-compulsive disorder, it is the performance of compulsions. Patients with both phobias and obsessive-compulsive disorder, Meyer found, can be cured through repeated exposure to the fear with prevention of the escape response.

In the present day, behavior therapy is almost always conducted in an outpatient setting rather than a hospital. The

131

critical steps are: (1) recording in a diary the severity and duration of all obsessions and compulsions as they occur throughout the day, (2) listing possible situations that would provoke obsessions, ranked according to the degree of anxiety that each would cause, and then (3) exposing oneself to various fearful situations while resisting the performance of compulsions.

An example is the case of Lisa, a thirty-year-old woman who developed the obsessional fear that her skin would be damaged by accidental exposure to a chemical found in beauty products called "alpha hydroxy." Fears of workplace contamination with the chemical had caused Lisa to quit her job as a salesclerk. By the time I first saw her, she seldom ventured out of her house.

Lisa and I met once a week. The worst of her obsessions was the thought that that she had directly touched an object tainted with alpha hydroxy. Others included the idea that she was dangerously near a store that sold products containing the chemical, and the idea that she had accidentally touched the face of someone who had used such an item. Her compulsions included washing her hands more than eighty times each day, repeatedly cleaning her floors, and, on occasions when she ventured out of her house, keeping her hands held tightly by her side.

Lisa made a list of various possible situations that could trigger her obsessional thoughts. This "OCD-situations hierarchy" is the key to structured behavioral therapy. At the top of her list, of course, was directly applying a product containing alpha hydroxy to her skin. Next was walking anywhere near a pharmacy. Not too anxiety-producing, but still requiring courage, would be to simply look at an advertisement of a beauty product that contained the substance.

Lisa began daily homework assignments. To start, she looked at anxiety-provoking pictures in magazines and refrained from washing for two hours. Enduring the anxiety that ensued, she discovered that nothing bad occurred. With encouragement, she moved up the hierarchy of situations, accomplishing more and more difficult tasks. After about three months, she was able to directly apply beauty products to her skin. Her hand washing had decreased to fifteen to twenty times a day, and she was walking freely outside her house. Soon she was able to get another job.

Such an excellent outcome is common when uncomplicated obsessive-compulsive disorder is treated with structured behavioral therapy. The process is straightforward. The skill of the therapist lies primarily in helping patients identify obsessions and compulsions, presenting the principles of therapy, and finding ways to persuade the patient to engage in exposure and response-prevention exercises.

Cognitive Therapy

While behavior therapy directs a person to act in certain ways that are therapeutic, such as exposing oneself to fearful situations, cognitive therapy aims to help a person find healthier ways to perceive upsetting thoughts. The process involves: (1) identifying the specific maladaptive ideas that cause a person difficulty, and then (2) changing the way that he or she views these thoughts so they become less upsetting. Like behavior therapy, cognitive therapy doesn't waste time delving into the past or trying to solve life problems. It too can lead to remarkable therapeutic changes in a short period of time.

Cognitive therapy was first introduced as a treatment for depression. In the late 1960s, psychiatrist Aaron Beck of the University of Pennsylvania traced people's low moods to self-defeating "automatic assumptions" that surfaced reflexively in specific situations. One such assumption might be "I'll never be able to complete this work"; another, "I'm so ugly that nobody likes me." Even though often completely unreasonable, such ideas would remain unchallenged by the individual. Beck

133

demonstrated that automatic assumptions could be modified by therapy, and that when this was accomplished a person's mood improved.

Beck was highly skilled in the use of a technique called "Socratic dialogue." He would calmly and persistently question the logic of his patients' depressive assumptions, leading them to find more healthy and adaptive ways to look at themselves. Subsequent research demonstrated that this approach could work as well or even better than antidepressant medications, and Beck's cognitive therapy for depression remains a highly popular treatment.[2]

Almost in parallel to Beck's work, Albert Ellis, a clinical psychologist in New York City, developed a form of cognitive therapy targeted primarily to anxiety disorders, called "rational emotive therapy" or RET. Ellis's genius was in identifying ten common "irrational beliefs" that fueled worry and self-doubt (e.g., "I must have love and approval from all the people I find significant"). In therapy, Ellis would focus on the belief that best explained the person's anxiety, challenge the patient to prove its validity, then encourage the patient to replace it with a more healthy belief (e.g., "It would be nice to have approval from everyone, but I can live without it"). Research studies have demonstrated the effectiveness of this approach, and Ellis went on to publish a number of popular books.[3] By the 1980s rational emotive therapy had become perhaps the most widely used type of psychotherapy for anxiety states in America.

Obsessive-compulsive disorder has always been especially intriguing to cognitive psychologists because for the sufferers of this particular disorder the thought itself is the complaint. For many years, however, experts believed that obsessions and compulsions were resistant to cognitive therapy. Since obsessional patients already knew that their upsetting thoughts were irrational, the thinking went, to emphasize the point served no purpose.

Studies conducted in the early 1990s, however, demonstrated that cognitive therapy can indeed be used to treat obsessive-compulsive disorder. The first came from psychologist Paul Emmelkamp in the Netherlands, who employed a variant of Ellis's rational emotive therapy to modify irrational beliefs that occur immediately after an obsession strikes, such as "It's terrible that I had that thought."[4] Other demonstrations soon followed that employed the basic principles of Beck's cognitive therapy.[5]

The key, therapists found, is that the therapeutic intervention has to cause a lasting revision in a person's outlook. It is clear, for instance, that simple reassurance is of no help. To tell a compulsive washer, "Don't worry, your hands are clean," does nothing to lessen the strength of her contamination fear the next time it strikes. What is necessary, rather, is that a patient learn to seriously question the validity of an obsessive fear so that when it next occurs less anxiety is triggered.

One of the first obsessive-compulsives I ever treated at Penn State was a devoutly Jewish student who related to me an interesting experience he had had in sixth grade. While eating his lunch in the school cafeteria one day, he had heard a few of his Christian friends talking about what happens to sinners who end up in hell. Subsequently, he himself became tormented by the thought that he would go to hell for contaminating their food. He began to engage in lengthy washing rituals and eventually completely avoided eating lunch in the school. One day he confided his problem to his father, who told him simply, "We're Jewish. We don't believe in hell." The patient's obsessions instantly disappeared, and obsessive-compulsive symptoms did not resurface until he devolped contamination fears a half a dozen years later. Why was the father's intervention effective? In his brief but elegant confrontation of his son's irrational thought, the father found a way to put his son's fear in an entirely new perspective. He did not just dismiss the obsession by saying "That's a crazy thought!" or offer immediate reassurance,

135

"Don't worry, you're not going to hell." He changed the assumptions that underlay the obsession. Cognitive psychologists call this "cognitive restructuring."

Two recent books attest to the current popularity of the cognitive approach. Jeffrey Schwartz's best-selling OCD self-help book *Brain Lock* sets out a powerful method for dealing with obsessional fears at the moment they occur. Schwartz, a psychiatrist at UCLA, advises patients to use a four-step procedure that involves the relabeling, reattributing, refocusing, and revaluing of each obsession.[6] The most recent book of Harvard OCD expert Lee Baer, *The Imp of the Mind*, describes recently developed cognitive techniques. One, for example, is called "calculating the probability of danger." Here, the therapist asks a series of structured questions that are designed to force patients to reassess the probability of their fear being realized.[7]

Suppose a patient suffers from the obsession that he or she will contract AIDS from germs on his or her hands. The therapist would ask questions such as the following: When the obsession strikes, what does the likelihood seem to be that your hands are contaminated? Right now, thinking as logically as you can, what do you think the chances are? What are the chances after you have washed once? If germs were on your hands, what are the chances they would get in your bloodstream? If they did get in your bloodstream, what are the chances you would get sick from them? If you got sick, what are the chances it would be serious? Multiplying together the suggested likelihoods for all of these questions yields an extraordinarily low chance of actually contracting AIDS. The patient is then asked to reflect on the huge difference between the probability that occurs to him or her when the obsession strikes and the true likelihood.

Although cognitive therapy appears to work well in the majority of cases of obsessive-compulsive disorder, it is widely believed by experts to be not quite as effective, overall, as behavior therapy. One of its shortcomings is in the treatment of religious obsessions. Albert Ellis's rational emotive therapy, for instance, rests on convincing a patient that an upsetting belief is irrational. By Ellis's standards, most all religious beliefs are irrational. Unless the therapist wishes to argue that religion itself is best abandoned (which some RET therapists do), this issue can bring therapy to a standstill. Techniques such as calculating the probability of danger are also frequently ineffective in this context. The chances that one will go to hell, or that one has displeased God (the two most common religious obsessions among Christians), are not readily open to such analysis.

Fortunately, the potential for developing new techniques in cognitive therapy is limited only by the capacity of the human mind to find useful ways of looking at things. As stated by Oxford's Paul Salkovskis, what cognitive therapy involves is simply "helping the patient to adopt an entirely different and more helpful perspective on obsessions."[8] The most helpful perspective, in some situations, may not be the most logical or rational. We will return to this idea at the end of this chapter.

Examining the Advice Given to Saints with OCD

As we have seen, Martin Luther, John Bunyan, and Saint Thérèse all received various sorts of counsel on how to deal with their obsessional fears. Most of it, unfortunately, was bad. Martin Luther's spiritual director in the Augustinian monastery, Dr. Staupitz, the only Catholic priest Luther continued to love and respect for his entire life, told Luther bluntly that he simply did not understand him. John Bunyan's experience with the "ancient Christian" was memorable. Telling Bunyan that yes, he probably had lost his salvation, permanently cured him of seeking help from others. Thérèse had some good advice, but most of it was bad. On one occasion when she shared her tormenting fears with Fr. Almire Pichon, her primary director, he simply forbade her to think such thoughts. Clearly, this represents "anti-exposure" advise. After Thérèse had found her

137

Little Way, she eloquently summed up her experiences with spiritual directors: "When the occasion came to open my soul, I received so little understanding that I said to God: 'From now on don't send me any more messengers who don't know how to tell me what I desire!'"[9]

We have previously touched on the cases of apparent obsessive-compulsive disorder suffered by three other great Christian figures: Ignatius of Loyola, Jane de Chantal, and Alphonsus Liguori. These individuals also both sought out spiritual advice for dealing with their tormenting thoughts and tried out various strategies on their own. It's instructive to see how they fared.

Ignatius of Loyola, the Spanish mystic who founded the Jesuit order in the sixteenth century, suffered an acute bout of obsessive-compulsive disorder in his early thirties that lasted about two years. Ignatius's primary obsession was that he harbored unconfessed sins. "I began to look for some spiritual man who would cure me of my scruples," he writes in his autobiography.[10] The first priest he consulted suggested writing out all the sins he could remember. Yet, Ignatius tells us, "the scruples returned, each time becoming more minute." It is clear why this approach backfired: rather than limiting his compulsive confessing (response prevention), Ignatius had been advised to compulsively enumerate his sins even more.

Next, Ignatius was counseled "not to confess anything of [his] past life unless it was something absolutely clear." This directive was also unhelpful, because when in the grips of his obsession, the tormenting thought that he had sinned "was quite clear." This was the equivalent of telling a person who checks the stove a hundred times a day to check it only if he or she is absolutely sure it is not shut off. Such counsel could easily lead to even more obsessing about the state of the stove. Not surprisingly, Ignatius gave up seeking advice.

His story, however, ends happily. Because of his strong willpower and extraordinary analytical abilities—perhaps also because he suffered only a relatively mild case of OCD—Ignatius discovered for himself an effective and behaviorally sound method of treatment. His self-styled approach was, in fact, similar to how a clinical psychologist might treat his case in the present day. First, Ignatius became "very clear on the matter" that his scruples were causing him "much harm." He then strongly made up his mind "never to confess past sins again" under any circumstances. The impressive result was that he soon "remained free of those scruples."

Several years later, Ignatius had a flare-up of obsessive-compulsive disorder when he happened to touch the hand of a sick man. Suddenly, he experienced the tormenting thought that he had contracted the Black Plague. "So strong did this fancy become," Ignatius writes, "that I could not control it." His hand actually began to hurt. In this situation, Ignatius employed a brilliant exposure and response-prevention exercise. He countered his irrational fear by thrusting his hand into his mouth and moving his fingers. He then told himself, "If you have the plague in your hand, now you'll also have it in your mouth!" After this, he relates, "My "imagination quieted down and the pain in my hand disappeared."[11]

After successfully treating his own obsessive-compulsive disorder, Ignatius counseled others on how to overcome similar problems. His approach to excessive worries about sin and compulsive confessing is set out most clearly in his famous *Spiritual Exercises* in a chapter entitled "Toward Perceiving and Understanding Scruples." It boils down to two principles. First, it is necessary to identify the source of a scruple (or obsession), that is, what exactly is causing the anxiety and disquiet. Secondly, one must oppose the scruple by acting in a manner contrary to it, such as stopping excessive confessions. Perhaps this great Catholic saint deserves to be called the first OCD behavioral therapist.

Jane de Chantal's case of obsessive-compulsive disorder is one of history's most fascinating. As discussed previously,

Saint Jane was a wealthy, highly talented, and energetic Renaissance nun who eventually founded her own religious order. At age twenty-nine she began to suffer from severe obsessions taking the form of blasphemous thoughts, "mental temptations and trials so severe," she writes, "that nothing in the wide world except death" could possibly provide relief.[12]

The man who would counsel her was none other than St. Francis de Sales, founder of the Salesian Order of priests. De Sales wrote the perennial Catholic best seller *An Introduction to the Devout Life,* and is known in Catholic circles as nothing less than the "father of spiritual direction." He penned an estimated 20,000 letters in his life, and many are examples of exquisitely caring and astute spiritual counseling. The most celebrated of all of his letters of direction, in fact, are those he wrote over a period of eighteen years to Jane de Chantal.[13] These letters are the topic of an entire volume in the distinguished series "Classics of Western Spirituality," and the subject of a recent book by Wendy Wright of the Weston School of Theology.

A review of the correspondence reveals, first of all, unwavering tenderness and compassion. One is struck by Francis's skill as a teacher. He expresses himself with great clarity and beauty, uses imaginative metaphors to help Jane understand herself better, and openly shares instances when he himself had suffered similarly. Yet it must also be said that the specific advice he gave her for her tormenting obsessions was worse than useless.

Concerning her blasphemous thoughts, he wrote, "You must make up your mind never to consent to them." As a result of this counsel, Jane made a vow "never voluntarily to look upon her temptations."[14] A sister of Jane remembered that in her worst moments she "was always imagining that she had either encouraged such temptations or consented to them."[15] Through his advice, Francis had actually laid the groundwork for Jane to suffer a prolonged obsessional struggle.[16] Attempting to repudiate her tormenting thoughts, we now know, would only make them come back stronger.

With time, Catholic spiritual direction for OCD sufferers improved. The writings of Ignatius became the standard. Several later priests offered insightful manuals that presaged even more accurately the concepts of modern behavior therapy. Perhaps the best of these is *The Directorium Asceticum*, written by the Jesuit John Baptist Scaramelli, in 1753.[17] As a result of such works, more Catholics tormented with religious obsessions received good advice.

Alphonsus Liguori is an example. St. Alphonsus, yet another great figure in the history of the Catholic church, founded the still flourishing Order of the Redemptorists in the eighteenth century and is known for his theological contributions to the church in the arena of moral theology. Although Alphonsus wrote sparingly about his symptoms, it is clear that he suffered from severe scrupulosity and compulsive confessing that began in adolescence and never completely abated. In Alphonsus's case, confessors gave good advice: they got him to stop his compulsions. "I have received the order never to confess past matters," Alphonsus writes. In reference to the daily recital of divine office he notes, "I have been ordered not to repeat the parts absent-mindedly . . . because it would open the way to scruples."[18] These were good behavioral interventions.

Liguori's fame in the Catholic church rests primarily on the fact that he reformed its teachings on sin, bringing to a halt a rigorist movement that had taken hold in Catholic teachings in the 1700s. Father Thomas Santa, an expert on both scrupulosity and the life of Alphonsus, writes that Liguori's scruples played a "pivotal role" in the development of his theology. The Redemptorist order that he founded continues a special outreach to those suffering from scrupulosity, publishing a regular newsletter, *Scrupulous Anonymous*, which has improved the lives of tens of thousands of Catholics with religious obsessions.[19]

141

Responsibility Modification Therapy

The last chapter reviewed an impressive array of evidence supporting an insight first made by Oxford psychologist Paul Salkovskis in 1987: "In obsessive-compulsive disorder, intrusive thoughts are mistakenly interpreted as indicating that a person may be responsible for harm to self or others." This remarkably perceptive observation has not been ignored by clinicians.

Over the last decade, a number of leading OCD experts, including Patricia Van Oppen, Mark Freeston, and Stanley Rachman, have proposed specific clinical approaches that are referred to as "responsibility modification strategies." The goal of these techniques, as of all cognitive therapies, is to modify dysfunctional beliefs and attitudes. Here, however, the emphasis is specifically on identifying and changing beliefs that involve pathological feelings of excessive personal responsibility.

Most commonly, the techniques involve actively challenging a person's "responsibility assumptions." In one procedure, the total responsibility for an obsessional fear is represented as a pie chart. The patient must consider all the possible factors that might play a part if the obsessional fear were realized, and assign them pieces of the pie. A patient who suffers the obsession that a fire will start in her gas stove, for instance, finds upon applying the pie chart that responsibility lies not only with her, but also with the stove's safety device, its gas-delivery system, and other members of her family. Although OCD sufferers tend to think they are 100 percent responsible for a feared outcome, a careful analysis of each factor involved forces them to reassess their own role.

Another technique involves contesting a patient's "double standard." The patient would blame herself if a fire started, but would she hold another person equally responsible? Almost certainly not. The therapist, making use of Socratic dialogue, helps the obsessional to fully grasp the irrational degree of personal responsibility that she takes upon herself, and to confront it. Similarly, yet another procedure assigns to the patient the role of a prosecuting attorney. In a mock court trial, she must "prove" her own guilt for allowing a fire to start on the basis of solid empirical evidence. Guided by the therapist, the patient comes to fully appreciate the error in her thinking.

Another procedure works by transferring accountability to someone else. In an experiment performed by researchers at the University of Vancouver, thirty OCD patients were visited in their homes and asked to expose themselves to their most frightening obsessional situations. A woman who feared that a fire would start in her stove, for example, was asked to turn her stove on and then off, then walk into the next room without checking it. This was accomplished under two different experimental conditions. In the first, the experimenter solemnly promised that if a fire started, she would neither be blamed for it nor charged for any damages. In the second, the experimenter told her that she had responsibility for anything bad that might occur. The results were striking. OCD sufferers who were assigned no responsibility experienced markedly less discomfort and fewer urges to check.[20] As Rachman notes, "A person who has been tormented for years by the need to conduct meticulous, repeated, slow checks of each use of the gas stove may revert within minutes to completely normal use of the stove—if he/she agrees to transfer of responsibility."[21]

Such direct transfer of responsibility might be the most powerful of all therapeutic approaches to obsessive-compulsive disorder. Unfortunately, it has shortcomings. For one thing, an individual willing to assume responsibility is not always available. For another, therapists generally strive to help their patients be more, not less, self-reliant.

For these reasons, when therapists do employ the tactic of transferring responsibility, the transfer is usually made to the therapist, and for only a short time. A patient monitors his thoughts, behaviors, and reactions when responsibility is transferred to the therapist, and then compares them to those that occurred when he held himself accountable. This exercise is usually repeated several times, and the results of the patient's self-monitoring are carefully examined.

Therapists have thus far not considered the direct transfer of responsibility in the context of religious faith. In the case of a believer, why couldn't responsibility be given to God? Indeed, as we shall see, this was the cure that was found by Luther, Bunyan, and Thérèse. It will be explored in the next chapter.

Transferring Responsibility to God

The Cure of Luther, Bunyan, and Thérèse

Martin Luther, John Bunyan and Thérèse of Lisieux share many similarities. As young adults, all three were, as William James said of Bunyan, "sensitive of conscience to a diseased degree."[1] Passing ideas that are normal for all Christians—a thought against God, doubt of a sacred truth, remembrance of a sin unconfessed—would crush them with anxiety and guilt. Fearing their salvation imperiled, all three engaged in time-consuming and disruptive rituals. Luther angered his superiors with marathon confessions; Bunyan wasted hours a day monotonously repeating Bible verses; and Thérèse compulsively sought reassurances.

All three sought to cure their anxieties through the conventional teachings of their respective Christian communities. These teachings, however, could not quell their fears. After years of enduring torment, each developed a highly individualistic religious philosophy that differed radically from the accepted view. Luther's was so extreme that it incited a revolution. Bunyan's, as Monica Furlong noted, "took him far beyond the conventional waters of Puritanism."[2] Thérèse's, according to Ida Görres, encompassed "an ideal of Christian perfection that had been forgotten for centuries."[3]

The fact that Luther, Bunyan, and Thérèse all suffered from obsessive-compulsive disorder explains a great deal. Their symptoms, once puzzling to biographers and historians alike, now can be recognized as typical obsessions and compulsions. Their inability to find consolation in common Christian practices such as confession and the recitation of Bible verses is explained by the fact that obsessions are immune to the sorts of reassurance that nonobsessive people find most helpful. That all three of these giants were misunderstood by their spiritual advisers is not surprising, because OCD causes behaviors so strange that they bewilder most who observe them. Finally, Luther, Bunyan, and Thérèse all developed mature religious philosophies that differed from those of their communities because (from a psychiatric standpoint) each needed desperately to find a cure for obsessions and compulsions and, in order to do so, needed to find an entirely new perspective from which to view obsessional fears.

There is yet another likeness between Luther, Bunyan, and Thérèse: that of their religious philosophies. Bunyan was raised in a purely Calvinistic environment, yet most theologians and historians agree with the observation of the eighteenth-century poet and philosopher S. T. Coleridge: "Bunyan may have been a [Calvinist] but I have met nothing in his writings that is not much more characteristically Lutheran."[4] Thérèse, despite never reading a word of Luther's writings (forbidden reading for all Catholics in nineteenth-century France), has actually been referred to as a Catholicized version of Luther. She found, according to French philosopher Jean Guitton, "the positive aspects of Luther's intuitive understanding of what was most important."[5]

Luther, Bunyan, and Thérèse lived in different centuries, couched their famous theologies in quite dissimilar terms, and fit their beliefs into the dogmas of Christian denominations that were poles apart. Yet, as has been noted by numerous theologians, their theologies are strikingly alike. Can obsessive-compulsive disorder account for this similarity?

Recent research demonstrating the central role of an excessive sense of personal responsibility in the genesis of obsessive-compulsive disorder provides a key to answering the question. For the purposes of this book, these magnificent theologies can be viewed as forms of responsibility modification therapy. Luther's *sola fide* (by faith alone), Bunyan's covenant theology, and Thérèse's Little Way can be seen as variations on a single "therapy" that works by giving the responsibility for all obsessional fears completely and absolutely to God.

Modifying Responsibility by Faith Alone

Luther's great insight in the tower of the Augustinian monastery at Erfurt was that he did not have to do anything to assure his salvation. God had imputed righteousness to him through a gratuitous act of mercy. Luther no longer needed to obsessively examine his behaviors to see if they were good enough. He no longer had to worry about confessing all his sins. He no longer needed to look at himself at all. He needed only to have faith in God's goodness. On that basis his eternal life was secure. "This is wonderful news to believe that salvation lies outside ourselves," Luther wrote. "I am justified and acceptable to God, although there are in me sin, unrighteousness, and horror of death."[6]

The psychoanalyst Erik Erikson likens the faith of Luther to the "basic trust of early infancy," a turning to God and a trusting

147

in his goodness, something like the absolute and unquestioning confidence an infant has in its mother.[7] Theologian John Dillenberger similarly writes that "Lutheran faith rests on apprehending the incomprehensible, gratuitous mercy of God."[8]

According to Richard Marius's penetrating psychological study, Luther's faith denotes "an attitude of heart and mind that leaves everything to God in the way that we might trust a promise from a loving father even when that father is distant from us and we have no visible proof that the promise will be kept." Thus, Marius concludes tellingly, faith alone worked for Luther because it "translates responsibility to God."[9]

Luther provides clear advice on how to handle the tormenting anxieties that we now recognize as obsessive-compulsive disorder in a letter to Barbara Lisskirchen, a member of his congregation who suffered from severe obsessions concerning her eternal destiny. How could she know for certain, Lisskirchen wondered, that she would go to heaven?

In his response to Frau Lisskirchen, Luther stresses the importance of overcoming such worries by turning them over to God and simply having faith in him. "Learn to say," he concludes, "Away with you Devil, you want to compel me to care for myself, when God everywhere says that I should let him care for me, declaring: 'I care for you; depend upon me.'"[10]

Luther came to believe that Christians can do nothing at all to assure their salvation. His views on the matter are most clearly revealed in a debate with Erasmus of Rotterdam, the leading Catholic intellectual of the sixteenth century. Erasmus insisted—reasonably enough, it would seem—that people have the power to choose to do good or evil, and thus influence their eternal destiny. Luther rejected this assertion. "In matters pertaining to salvation or damnation," Luther wrote, "a man has no free choice, but is a captive, subject, and slave either of the will of God or the will of Satan."[11]

The crucial role of excessive personal responsibility sheds light on why, psychologically speaking, Luther was drawn to this conclusion. Marius, again, writes perceptively on this point. The goal of Erasmus in his debate with Luther, Marius observes, was to "vindicate the conviction that human beings are responsible for their actions."[12] Luther, on the other hand, "thought that to place any responsibility for salvation on himself was to plunge himself back into that world where he believed that he must combat reason with his own strength."[13] Luther writes in one of his most highly regarded (and controversial) works, *Bondage of the Will*,

> I do not want free will. . . . I should be forced to labor with no guarantee of success, and to beat my fists at the air. If I lived and worked to all eternity, my conscience would never reach comfortable certainty as to how much it must do to satisfy God.[14]

Luther even went so far as to say that we must keep our faith in God even in the absence of absolute certainty that we will go to heaven. "We should trust the grace of God," Luther wrote to a friend, "but remain uncertain of the future perseverance."[15] In other words, as he writes elsewhere, "God is good even if he should send all men to perdition."[16] For Luther, it was Christ's suffering and dying for us that was the proof of God's unfailing love. Our part was to give to God the responsibility for anything that could possibly happen, and simply trust in him. This is, indeed, a radical and difficult type of faith. Such strong medicine was required to release Luther from his terrifying obsessions.

Never was Luther drawn to any of the newer theological approaches of the Catholic church of his day that, one might think, could have offered him another way out of his suffering. The mysticism of the popular fourteenth-century Dominican writer and preacher John Tauler, for example, stressed the importance of union with God through love. The humanistic philosophy of Erasmus suggested loving our brethren and not

149

worrying too much about difficult theological questions. Why could Luther not find a comfortable theological base for himself in such views? From a psychological perspective, no Christian construct in Luther's time was as specifically therapeutic for obsessions and compulsions as that which he discovered. Only *sola fide* was able to completely relieve the agonizing sense of accountability that Luther felt for his salvation. It accomplished this by transferring responsibility to God.

Jesus on the Judgment Seat: The Covenant Theology of John Bunyan

Bunyan's seventeenth-century England, even more than Luther's Germany, is known for its great diversity of Christian views. Dozens of different religious sects competed for converts. Ranters denied the authority of the Bible, while Muggletonians believed that reason was created by the devil. Quakerism, founded during Bunyan's lifetime by the mystic George Fox, offered a path of direct union with God within a Protestant framework. All of these represented clear alternatives to the Puritan theology that both nourished Bunyan in his youth and later ignited his obsessive-compulsive disorder, yet Bunyan wrote against them vehemently. Bunyan, like Luther, overcame his obsessions and compulsions only when he found a way to give God complete responsibility for his obsessional fear of eternal damnation.

One might think that Protestants living in the 1600s would have been relatively free from religious obsessions. Luther, the father of Protestantism, had, after all, discovered a cure for them, and made it the cornerstone of his theology. In England during Bunyan's time, however, the major doctrinal figure was John Calvin, who had emphasized above all the doctrine of predestination. According to this belief, all who would be granted eternal life, and all who would be eternally damned, had been chosen by God before the beginning of time. Of all the Christian sects in England, the one that was most Calvinistic and predestinarian was that which nourished John Bunyan, the Puritans.

Puritans based their happiness in this world on their assurance that they were predestined to be saved. But how did they know? They were encouraged to take their disciplined moral efforts, for which they were well known, as proof. "The godly do good works," said the Puritan minister John Dod, "to assure and certify their consciousness of election."[17] What this represented, however, to a person with obsessive-compulsive disorder, could be a subtle return to "salvation by works," the very philosophy that had tormented Luther. Like Luther, Bunyan felt called to demonstrate his worthiness in order to secure certainty in his salvation. Like Luther, he could not handle such an awesome responsibility.

Bunyan himself credits Luther with leading him to the change that saved his sanity. Providentially, he stumbled across a tattered copy of Luther's *Commentary on Galatians*. "I found my condition," Bunyan recalls, "so largely and profoundly handled, it was as if his book had been written out of my heart." Bunyan came to value Luther's work as the most important after the Bible, preferring it "before all the books that ever I have seen as most fit for a wounded conscience."[18] Bunyan made Luther's *sola fide* a cornerstone of his own religious philosophy.

Luther had put the focus on God the Father; Bunyan centered it on the person of Jesus. In his mature version of what is referred to as covenant theology, Bunyan stresses the crucial importance of actively believing that Jesus steps in to take responsibility for us every time we sin. Jesus takes the blame, and as a result we remain completely spotless, or "righteous." As biographer Gordon Wakefield notes, "Here is the quintessence of Bunyan's theology; here are the texts which meant most to him: 'My grace is sufficient for thee' (2 Cor. 12:9) and 'Him that cometh to me I will in no way cast out' (John 6:37)."[19]

151

Just as money is put into the hands of trustees, Bunyan writes, so God has put our salvation "into the hands of the trusty Jesus."[20] The last words of his spiritual autobiography read, "The wisdom of God doth order [my corruptions] for my good . . . they show me the necessity of flying to Jesus [and] provoke me to look to God through Christ to carry me through this world."

Bunyan's theology has, perhaps, a certain appeal to the imagination that Luther's lacks, with its constant invocation of the image of Jesus. Bunyan stresses the importance of actively picturing Jesus in heaven, forcefully intervening on our behalf, taking the brunt of the Father's wrath.

In her insightful biography *Puritan's Progress*, Monica Furlong, fully recognizing that Bunyan suffered from some sort of serious psychological illness, frames a compelling question. Furlong writes,

> The greatest difficulty in understanding the thought of a man like Bunyan is in grasping the role that Christ played in his mind. That he is of supreme and therapeutic importance to him we have his own words over and over again, yet quite how the therapy worked, or "who" as you might say, he is to him, is a puzzling and not entirely soluble problem.[21]

The problem is now solvable. Bunyan's obsessions revolved around the theme that he was displeasing to God, which meant the loss of his salvation and "hellfire." The healing power of Christ for Bunyan, in regard to his obsessive-compulsive disorder, came when Bunyan saw Christ as a person to whom he could give responsibility for pleasing God. The Puritans, according to historian Ernst Bacon, "lived their lives with a keen sense of responsibility to the Almighty."[22] Bunyan, finally, was able to give all the responsibility back to the "Almighty" through Christ.

Another interesting discovery by modern cognitive psychologists may also have bearing here. "Thought-action fusion" refers to a tendency to believe that what is depicted in a thought is happening in reality. For example, a person may suddenly have the idea that a loved one has been in an accident. If thought-action fusion takes place, he or she will be drawn to believe that the accident has actually occurred in spite of there being no factual basis for drawing that conclusion. A handful of studies, mostly employing psychological tests, have provided tantalizing evidence that thought-action fusion is especially correlated with obsessive-compulsive disorder.

Bunyan gives numerous vivid descriptions of the unusual manner by which ideas grabbed hold of him. Indeed, they could shatter his consciousness, literally bringing him breathless to his knees. W. R. Owens comments on the strange "power of Biblical texts over Bunyan's mind."[23] Often, passages took the form of overpowering obsessions that tormented Bunyan "like masterless hell-hounds." At other times, however, biblical verses brought him an ecstatic sense of peacefulness and joy. "This made a strange seizure on my spirit," Bunyan writes of one such verse. "It brought light with it, and commanded a silence in my heart."[24] Thought-action fusion may help explain why, in Furlong's words, Christ assumed for Bunyan such a "supreme and therapeutic importance."

Indeed, Luther and Thérèse also appear to have possessed this tendency. When Thérèse, as an adolescent, suffered the obsession that she had lied about her "strange illness," the tormenting thought became so strong that she was strongly drawn to believe it was true, despite endless assurances to the contrary. In the case of Luther, thought-action fusion may help clarify the circumstances of his famous "tower experience." Some biographers have questioned whether, as Luther recounts, his discovery of *sola fide* could really have occurred at once as a sudden blinding breakthrough. "It seems more plausible," Marius writes, "that like most sudden insights it was not something utterly new . . . that the discovery grew over a period of months or years."[25] But an understanding of

153

thought-action fusion makes a "blinding breakthrough" seem more believable. For Luther, the sudden idea that he was saved was, perhaps, something like being abruptly transported from the midst of a war zone to a tropical paradise.

Is there a message here for psychiatrists and psychologists? Obsessive-compulsive disorder sufferers, at times, think differently than other people. It is the pathological aspect of their thinking that is the subject of clinical inquiry. Yet there is, quite possibly, a powerfully creative aspect to their cognitive tendencies that we neglect, a creativity fueled by the unusually vivid real-life quality of certain of their thoughts. The lives of Luther, Bunyan, and Thérèse could be quickly transformed by the force of a new idea—for the better or for the worse. For Luther, Bunyan, and Thérèse, thoughts were not separate from life itself.

Blind Trust in God's Mercy: Thérèse and Her Little Way

Thérèse's nineteenth-century France was a hothouse for widely divergent Catholic views that ranged from ultraconservative Jansenism to liberal Quietism. Thérèse attended a Benedictine school, trained as a Carmelite nun, and received spiritual direction from a Jesuit—three different religious orders with differing spiritual emphases. What Thérèse was not familiar with was the theology of Luther or that of Bunyan. Yet on her own she developed an exquisite religious philosophy that is quite similar to theirs.

The great Swiss theologian Hans Urs von Balthasar has observed that Thérèse represents nothing less than the Catholic answer to Luther. Both, he writes, are one in their "clear-cut preference for New Testament mercy as against Old Testament justice," and in their "stress upon trusting fiducia" ("with the confidence of a formal contract") in the person of God as opposed to "good works."[26]

Saint Thérèse, like Luther and Bunyan, emphasized above all the transfer of responsibility. She tells us that, at a moment when she felt shattered by her tormenting doubts, "God lowered Himself to me, and instructed me secretly in the things of His love."[27] What God showed to her she called the Little Way, which she defined as "the way of trust and absolute surrender."[28] It is "to expect everything from God as a little child expects everything from its father."[29] For Thérèse, sanctity "consists in a disposition of heart which makes us humble and little in the arms of God."[30] "My way," she writes, "is all confidence and love."[31]

Thérèse's Little Way emphasizes more of a reciprocal relationship with God than the imputed grace of Bunyan and Luther. Her part was to remain as a child, giving God all the responsibility for her actions. She had to remain "little," because if she allowed herself to grow up God would look on her differently. "Even the poor," Thérèse explains, "give a child what is necessary, but as soon as he grows up, the father no longer wants to feed him and says, 'Work now, you can take care of yourself.'"[32] In contrast, Thérèse writes, "As soon as God sees us thoroughly convinced of our littleness, He extends his hand to us." Her closest friend in Carmel, her sister Céline, put it like this: "Thérèse turned her thoughts to the art of becoming smaller and smaller so that God would accept full responsibility for her."[33]

The Battle for Faith

Luther, Bunyan, and Thérèse all engaged in heroic struggles with obsessive-compulsive disorder. Biographers describe Luther as living "a life marked by battle raging within and without"; Bunyan as suffering "despairing agonies as he pored in terrifying isolation over his Bible"; and Thérèse as enduring "a continuous trial . . . the vise was only rarely and briefly loosened."[34] It is critical to emphasize the active and dynamic nature of the cure that each of these spiritual greats separately found.

Effective therapy for obsessions and compulsions always involves a fight. More than 30 percent of patients fail in behavior therapy, and the most common reason is a lack of will to fully face up to their fears. UCLA's Jeffrey Schwartz emphasizes the difficulty that is involved in willfully changing one's beliefs. "It's a war and the enemy is OCD," Schwartz writes. Yet, "the person with obsessive-compulsive disorder has a powerful weapon. It is the knowledge of what is true. He or she works constantly to prevent confusing the truth with the voice of obsessive-compulsive disorder."[35]

Luther, Bunyan, and Thérèse all stressed the extreme difficulty of holding on to the degree of faith that they attained. Luther said that faith is the most difficult of all works. Bunyan wrote, "Run for heaven, fight for heaven, labor for heaven, wrestle for heaven, or you are like to go without it. . . . He that undertakes to believe, sets upon the hardest task that ever was proposed to man . . . believing is sweating work."[36] Thérèse likened herself to a spiritual warrior. In a poem written in the last year of her life, she pledged to Jesus her greatest efforts.

> I have the powerful armor of the Warrior.
> If I imitate him and fight bravely . . .
> Then I can sing of the strength and sweetness
> Of your mercies. . . .
> Smiling, I bravely face the fire.
> And in your arms, O my Divine Spouse,
> I shall die singing on the battlefield
> My weapons in hand.[37]

The faith of Luther, Bunyan, and Thérèse, therefore, stands in contrast to religious philosophies that are passive in nature. Quietism, which achieved great popularity in the seventeenth-century Catholic church, emphasizes complete acceptance of all that happens. Many mystical and fatalistic philosophies, likewise, emphasize an attitude of resignation. Though such an attitude can at times be helpful for obsessive-compulsive disorder, because it reduces personal responsibility, passive resignation is not what Luther, Bunyan, and Thérèse came to believe in. They settled on a less popular and more difficult therapy, but one that was ultimately more powerful and more healing.

At first glance, the theology of Luther, Bunyan, and Thérèse sounds so simple and rewarding that one wonders why most Christians have not always embraced it. The difficulty lies in keeping faith, particularly when in "dark nights of the soul," God seems to disappear. It is an awesome task. Perhaps it sometimes takes obsessive-compulsive disorder to drive a person to this therapy of absolute trust in the power and mercy of the person of God.

A Therapy of Trust

Practical Use

We have seen that Martin Luther, John Bunyan, and Thérèse of Lisieux all appear to have suffered from what is now called obsessive-compulsive disorder. Further, that all three overcame it through faith that God would take all of the responsibility for their insistent fears. Lastly, it has been shown that this spiritual cure for OCD can be interpreted as a specific form of cognitive therapy.

It was faith alone that finally allowed Luther, Bunyan, and Thérèse to resolve their obsessional struggles. It is critical, however, to emphasize the distinctive nature of their faith. To Christians, the term often means an unquestioning belief in a theological doctrine, such as that scripture is infallible. The faith that cures OCD, however, is somewhat different. Rather than commitment to a principle or an idea, it is trust in a person, the person of God.

Such faith, or trust, does not guarantee that nothing bad will happen. Suppose an individual with obsessions that her stove will catch fire decides to check it only once and then give the responsibility for harm to God. She feels, of course, a confident hope that God, in his mercy, will not allow her fear to be realized. Yet she does not know all of God's plans. Ultimately, she must simply trust that whatever God ordains is for the best. This is the type of faith that was found by Luther, Bunyan, and Thérèse: confidence that God will take care of those who turn to him, no matter what happens.

Different Christian truths address different psychological needs. One might suggest to a bereaved widow, for instance, that her husband is in a better place, in heaven. One might remind a guilt-ridden friend of the forgiveness that is found in the confession of sins. Not so clear is what is helpful for obsessional fears—that's why our church has had so much trouble dealing with them over the centuries. Fortunately, Luther, Bunyan, and Thérèse have pointed out to us a powerful truth that specifically speaks to the Christian sufferer of obsessive-compulsive disorder: God will always take responsibility for any fear that assails us, if we only turn to him with unconditional trust in his power and mercy.[1]

This chapter suggests some practical ways of putting to use this therapy of trust. It begins with a hands-on, three-step method for applying the therapy within a cognitive-behavioral therapy framework. The following sections include special prayers and Bible verses that OCD sufferers may find helpful, and answers to some of the questions commonly asked by Christian OCD sufferers who are thinking about getting treatment, such as: Is a therapist necessary? What sort of a therapist should I see? Should medications be used? In closing, the chapter reviews several fundamental Christian truths that underlie the therapy of trust.

A Basic Formula

From a psychological perspective the therapy of trust discovered by Luther, Bunyan, and Thérèse treats obsessive-compulsive disorder through "cognitive restructuring," the development of more healthy ways of thinking. It provides a new perspective from which to view obsessional fears that makes them less frightening.

Normally, the course of cognitive therapy as practiced today aims to challenge the rationality of an obsessional fear. The therapist teaches the OCD sufferer to question the truth of an obsession at the moment it strikes, and to replace it with a more logical and realistic assessment of the situation. In *Brain Lock*, for instance, UCLA's Jeffrey Schwartz suggests a practical four-step approach to cognitive therapy for obsessive-compulsive disorder. Whenever obsessions strike, the OCD suffer should: (1) Relabel tormenting thoughts as obsessions rather than realistic worries; (2) reattribute them to a biochemical misfiring in the brain; (3) refocus on a meaningful activity rather than trying to stop the obsession; and finally, (4) revalue the need to perform compulsions, which lessens as obsessions weaken. This is powerful therapy. Occasionally, my OCD patients are completely cured through the use of this deceptively simple approach.

In the therapy of trust, the emphasis is shifted. It is not the rationality of an obsessional fear that is questioned, but rather who should take responsibility for it. The following is a three-step method for Christian OCD sufferers to employ.

Step #1: Recognize obsessions when they strike

In order to put obsessions in proper perspective, one must first be able to quickly identify them. Fortunately, this is usually not difficult. Obsessional thoughts are intrusive, repetitive, completely unwanted, and recognized (at least in a moment of quiet reflection) as being inappropriate to be thinking. They possess a unique quality that psychiatrists refer to as "ego-alien": It is as if they come from outside one's normal sense of self. The natural reaction is to dismiss them from one's mind, yet they only come back stronger, at last provoking the desperate cry, "Why in heaven's name do I keep thinking these thoughts?"

My patients say that the easiest way to recognize obsessions is the intense, overwhelming pressure felt to put them right. As one student put it: "I know it's OCD when I respond to it like it's the most important thing in my life." Another student remarked: "I know it's OCD when I feel great urgency. I have to do something right now, because waiting could cause immense harm." There is a characteristic "feel" to obsessions. Once you know it, obsessions can be quickly and confidently identified.

Step #2: Transfer responsibility to God

Recent psychological research suggests that individuals suffer from obsessions because of an excessive sense of responsibility for harm to self or others. The tormenting thoughts can be put to rest when the responsibility for harm is transferred to another person. In the therapy of trust, the responsibility for the feared outcome of an obsession is transferred to God. A person suffering from fire obsessions, for instance, turns to God and allows him to take responsibility for the prevention of fire; a Christian tormented by contamination obsessions gives God the responsibility for whether or not he will get a disease; an individual who fears he has offended God leaves responsibility for any offense to God.

Sometimes the focus of fear is not completely obvious. A student of mine, for instance, suffered the obsessional idea that she would jump out of her fourth-floor dorm window. It turned out, surprisingly, that she was not particularly afraid of the act of jumping, or even of dying. Rather, it was that her parents would be devastated if she did. In applying the therapy of trust to this case, therefore, what would be transferred to God would be the responsibility for her parents' feelings.

Most of us are familiar with the image of Jesus found in Revelation: "Behold, I stand at the door and knock" (3:20 KJV).

This is a helpful picture to keep in mind when employing the therapy of trust. We simply invite Jesus into our lives, share our obsessional fear with him, and give him the responsibility for it: "Here, Jesus, you look after this."

It is also helpful to remember Mary's words to Jesus at the wedding in Cana. Mary, acting just like an OCD sufferer, first takes responsibility on herself for the fact that the wine has run out. In order to deal with this situation, she simply turns to Jesus and says, "They have no wine" (John 2:3 KJV). Then she goes away and leaves Jesus alone. She doesn't press the point or repeat it; she doesn't demand proof that he will get more wine, or even that he has heard her. This is what the obsessive-compulsive must do: simply leave the matter to Jesus.

Step #3: Prove your trust; resist compulsions

Compulsions are acts done over and over to lessen the anxiety of an obsession. OCD sufferers need to make a concerted effort to lessen their performance of compulsions, because they consume time, cause embarrassment, injure health, and in the long run cause obsessions to become even stronger. For Christians, there is yet another reason to limit compulsions: to prove their trust in God.

When Luther said that we are saved by faith alone, he did not mean that we are relieved from exerting great effort in our lives. "Demonstrate by your works that you have faith," he writes.[2] "Don't be lazy or idle. Get busy and work."[3] Saint Thérèse puts it this way: "We must prove our love by all the good works of which we are capable."[4] Christians with OCD must work to resist compulsions. In doing so they demonstrate or prove, both to God and to themselves, how much they trust him and love him.

On a practical level, one cannot spend all day in a frenzy battling compulsions. What I recommend to my patients is trying to win small victories over OCD a couple of times every day: by shortening the amount of time spent on a ritual by a few minutes, or, even better, by postponing it for fifteen minutes. When an obsessional fear strikes and you are drawn to perform compulsions, try telling yourself: "Right now it is more important for me to trust in God than to make certain that my fear does not come true."

Daily Prayers and Bible Verses

Luther, Bunyan, and Thérèse all prayed for lengthy periods every day; and the therapy of trust requires a great deal of prayer. Transferring responsibility to God is itself a form of prayer. It must be kept in mind, however, that some degree of caution must be employed by OCD sufferers in the use of prayers. They can easily turn into compulsions that make obsessive-compulsive disorder worse.

The Bible provides the key to understanding when prayer becomes compulsive. In Matthew 6:7 Jesus explains: "When you pray, do not use vain repetitions as the heathen do. For they think that they will be heard for their many words" (NKJV). The New American Standard Bible translates "vain" as "meaningless." Compulsive prayers are rote incantations of words, done for no other reason than to put right an obsession. They do not reach out to God. They are, as the Bible tells us, self-centered and hollow. As a rule, OCD sufferers should strive to never repeat a private prayer more than once.

Especially likely to turn into compulsions are prayers directly asking God to prevent the feared outcome of an obsession. The woman who obsesses that a fire will start in her stove, for instance, prays to God to stop a fire from happening. The individual with a terrifying obsession to stab a loved one prays that God will prevent him from ever carrying out the dreadful act. While seemingly appropriate, these sorts of prayers are usually counterproductive.

In psychological terms, such prayers represent reassurance-seeking. The problem with reassurance is that it doesn't cause a lasting change in how one views an obsessional fear. When the same obsession next strikes, it is just as frightening, and reassurance is needed once again. What the Christian needs to do instead is turn to God in confidence and leave the obsessional fear with him. Such a prayer goes beyond a simple, self-centered request for reassurance.

The Apostle Paul writes in Second Corinthians, "a thorn in the flesh was given to me . . . I pleaded with the Lord three times that it might depart from me. And He said to me, 'My grace is sufficient for you, for My strength is made perfect in weakness'" (12:7 NKJV). Although no evidence suggests that Paul suffered from clinical obsessions, his remark applies perfectly to the sufferers of obsessive-compulsive disorder. There is no point in praying to God for relief from an obsessional fear. God wants us to accept our weakness and depend on him.

It should be noted that some obsessions strike precisely when one is praying: "God didn't hear me," "I didn't say my prayer with enough sincerity," "I forgot an important word," "What if I was actually praying to Satan?" All such doubts and fears must be recognized as obsessions themselves. They lead away from God. Strive to ignore them.

A morning prayer. It is good for anyone fighting obsessive-compulsive disorder to start the day with a battle plan. I recommend to my patients that they pick one particularly troublesome obsession and picture how they will deal with it later by transferring to God the responsibility for it and bearing the anxiety that will follow. Also helpful is a prayer that asks God for the strength to carry this plan out, such as the following.

Jesus, I know that you stand at the door and knock. You, who have authority over all things in heaven and earth, long to come into my life and help me. Lord, I feel helpless to deal with the obsessions that take control of me. Let your Holy Spirit strengthen me today so that when obsessions occur, I can give to you all of the responsibility for them. Help me, Jesus, with my lack of trust, and provide me with courage to resist compulsions.

Bible verses. Luther, Bunyan, and Thérèse were not only great prayers, they were devoted to God's word as it is revealed in scripture. Martin Luther discovered the faith that cured his obsessive-compulsive disorder while meditating on the meaning of Romans 1:17: "He who through faith is righteous shall live" (RSV). He finally came to realize that the passage did not imply that only those who are able to make themselves righteous will live eternally. Rather, it meant that God grants the righteousness necessary for salvation to those he chooses through a gift of faith. This realization changed Luther's life and the lives of millions.

Thérèse also discovered her true path to God while pondering scripture passages. When she was twenty, her sister Céline joined her in the Carmelite monastery, bringing along a handwritten copy of much of the Bible's Old Testament. Up to that point, Thérèse, although an avid reader, had never examined some of these writings—not surprising since the Catholic church of that era discouraged young nuns from reading parts of the Old Testament. Thérèse felt no compunctions, however, about reading her sister's notes, and soon found herself in awe of certain passages. Two of them, in particular, spoke to her deeply: "Whoever is a little one, let him come to me" (Prov. 9:4) and "As one whom a mother caresses, so will I comfort you" (Isa. 66:13).[5] These two verses awakened in Thérèse the realization that she did not need to climb a difficult staircase of perfection in order to please God. All she needed to do was to remain little and trust absolutely in his mercy.

Thérèse came to treasure many other Bible verses that reflected God's special love for little ones. Some of her other favorites were: "The Lord shall gather up the little lambs, and take them up in his bosom" (Isa. 40:11); "Suffer the little children to come unto me, for such is the kingdom of heaven" (Matt. 19:14); "As a father has compassion on his children, so has the Lord compassion on us" (Ps. 103:13); "In truth I tell you, anyone who does not welcome the kingdom of God like a little child will never enter it" (Mark 10:15). Thérèse copied passages such as these on a card, and kept it with her.

John Bunyan, like all Puritans, was fervently devoted to scripture. During the life-changing numinous experience in which he perceived the closeness of Jesus Christ, two texts were revealed to him in their full meaning: "My grace is sufficient for thee" (2 Cor. 12:9) and "Him that cometh to me I will in no wise cast out" (John 6:37 KJV).

The case of Bunyan, however, also illustrates a special difficulty that can arise when OCD sufferers use Bible verses. Some of the passages he memorized became fearful obsessions; others he used as compulsions. When Bunyan's OCD was at its worst, he could spend hours a day involved in a giant battle of Bible verses.

Given the value to Christians of memorizing and frequently calling to mind Bible verses, the OCD sufferer must exert some degree of care in their use. As noted, the Bible specifically warns against vain or meaningless repetitions (Matt. 6:7). What is important in using a verse is to focus on its full meaning, and not to reduce it to mere words to be repeated.

Planned Exposure and Response-Prevention Exercises

Psychologically speaking, the therapy of trust described thus far represents primarily a form of "cognitive restructuring," that is, changing the way people think about their obsessional fears. The therapy can be extended, however, to include the remarkably useful exercise that lies at the heart of traditional behavioral therapy: "exposure and response-prevention." Here, an individual purposefully brings to mind a chosen obsession, and then refrains from performing compulsions for up to two hours. The result is rapid habituation to the obsessional fear. In difficult cases of OCD, structured exposure and response-prevention is often necessary for the best outcome. Fortunately, this powerful behavioral treatment fits very well into the therapy of trust. It could be called, "Prove Your Trust, Part II."

The reader will remember that the key step in behavior therapy is the construction of a graded list of situations that can provoke obsessional fears. Usually, the situations involve simply going somewhere or performing a task. For the individual with contamination obsessions, the list might contain items such as "rub my hand along a railing," "enter a public bathroom," or "touch the inside of a trash can." For the person with religious obsessions, it might include "enter a church," "read a certain Bible verse," or "watch a movie that deals with Satan." Sometimes, however, people are best exposed to obsessional fears through exercises of the imagination. These can run from writing a story in which an obsessional fear comes true to telling oneself an obsession is actually happening.

Unfortunately, there is a special difficulty that can arise in the use of exposure and response-prevention with devout individuals: The very situations that might be most therapeutic may be regarded as sinful.

Such was the case with Mark, a bright graduate student in computer science, who presented with complaints of "religious thoughts" that jumped into his mind, such as "I don't actually believe that Jesus is my Savior," "I'm going to hell," and "I want to sell my soul to the devil." In order to right his obsessional fears, Mark was praying compulsively, confessing excessively to campus priests, and spending hours a day attempting to reassure himself that he did not actually believe what he was thinking.

Mark quickly learned the essential facts about obsessive-compulsive disorder and how it can be treated. When he heard about exposure and response-prevention, he was eager to try

168

it. Mark found it difficult to come up with specific situations or tasks that would provoke his obsessional thoughts. Finally, he developed a list of imagined exposures that were quite challenging: "Write out 'I want to sell my soul to the devil,'" "Say out loud 'I want to sell my soul to the devil,'" "Record on a loop tape 'I want to sell my soul,' and play it over and over," and "Write a story in which I actually do give in and sell my soul to the devil." The problem, however, was that Mark decided he couldn't try any of these exposure exercises, because to do so might be sinful.

I assured Mark that performance of the exercises would not imply that he actually wanted to sell his soul to the devil; it was simply a way of bringing his obsessional thoughts to mind so he could habituate to their fear. What Mark needed to do was to give himself permission—just during the "formal" exercise—to perform an act that outwardly seemed sinful to him but in truth was not.

Mark consulted a priest about the matter, and the priest wisely explained to him that his blasphemous thoughts were like obscenities yelled by a stranger. Mark could not help but hear them, but he was not responsible for them. He did not sin simply because they registered on his mind. The priest told Mark that purposefully exposing himself to his blasphemous obsessions would not necessarily be sinful. It would be the equivalent of his purposefully exposing himself to people yelling obscenities, which would not represent a sin if it was for a greater good. (I was shocked by the excellence of this advice; I wondered if the priest had suffered OCD himself.)

Mark proceeded to carry out behavior therapy exercises almost every day. First he whispered to himself, "I want to sell my soul to the devil." Whenever tempted to compulsively reassure himself that he didn't really want to, he whispered the sentence again. After a while, he found the task easy. Next he said the sentence out loud. Finally, after a few weeks, he was able to write this sentence out and experience minimal anxiety.

Mark's exposure exercises took great courage. He explained, "I went to the deepest part of my mind and got every thought out, but it wasn't easy. I've experienced what God's mercy is. I've learned to trust in God: whatever happens, happens. God is good, and I can leave everything to him."

The use of formal exposure and response is always challenging. An OCD sufferer almost always needs help with the construction of a graded list of obsessional fears, and encouragement to persevere. As a rule, this form of treatment should not be attempted without professional help.

When to See a Therapist

Obsessive-compulsive disorder occurs in degrees of severity: mild, moderate, and severe. In mild cases, an individual is troubled by obsessions and compulsions, yet gets along satisfactorily in all aspects of life. In moderate cases, the symptoms are not only disturbing but disrupting. They interfere significantly with a person's ability to function normally in work, family, or social life. In severe cases, the ability to function normally may be lost. Appendix B contains the widely used "Y-BOCS" test, which provides a general gauge of the severity of obsessions and compulsions.

I recommend that anyone with more than a mild case of obsessive-compulsive disorder see a cognitive-behavioral therapist. OCD is not a condition to feel ashamed of and suffer silently. As discussed in chapter 6, it is a biomedical disorder, similar in many ways to high blood pressure. Two excellent treatments are available—cognitive-behavioral therapy and medications—and both can markedly help the great majority of OCD sufferers. The first to try is cognitive-behavioral therapy.

What sort of therapist to see? Devout Christians would ideally see a therapist who shares their faith. Few Christian counselors, however, are specifically trained in cognitive-behavior therapy for obsessive-compulsive disorder. Overall, I think it is more important to see an expert in the treatment of OCD than a therapist who is Christian. More than depression or generalized anxiety, the treatment of obsessions and compulsions requires specific training.

There are several good ways to find an excellent therapist. If you live near a teaching center, preferably a medical school's department of psychiatry or a university's department of psychology, call and ask if they have a specialist in obsessive-compulsive disorder, or, better yet, an OCD clinic. If they do, you can be reasonably assured of getting good treatment there.

If you don't live near a teaching center, contact the Obsessive-Compulsive Foundation, a national, nonprofit, nonpolitical advocacy group. The foundation keeps an up-to-date listing of OCD specialists and clinics throughout the world. Another good option: contact the leader of an OCD support group in your area for advice on a good therapist to see. There are more than two hundred active OCD groups in the United States and Canada, and a listing of them can be obtained through the OC Foundation or on the Web. If these methods fail, call psychiatrists, psychologists, social workers, or counselors in your area and ask them if they are specifically trained in cognitive-behavioral therapy for OCD. If they are not, ask them if they know someone who is.

Once the OCD sufferer has found a good cognitive-behavioral therapist, he or she can supplement standard treatment with the Christian approach discussed in this book. No OCD therapist I know would object. Good therapists actively encourage their patients to new ways of behaving and thinking that lead to therapeutic exposure and response-prevention. If by chance you have the bad luck to find a person who is antagonistic toward your Christian beliefs, abandon ship immediately.

Relying on the church community. It is important to get support from fellow Christians, yet I suggest being judicious regarding the people with whom one discusses one's symptoms. The

171

regrettable fact is that if you stand up in a group of Christians and confide your worst obsession, they are unlikely to understand, no matter how much you explain. This is especially true if the obsession deals with violence or sex. People just don't comprehend the nature of obsessive-compulsive disorder. Often it is better to simply ask for general prayers for your excessive fearfulness and anxiety, and leave it at that.

It can be critically important, however, to have a full discussion of your problem with your minister or priest. Not uncommonly, Christians with OCD are confused about what represents a sin and what does not. Harvard psychiatrist Bill Minichiello, who is both an expert on OCD and a Roman Catholic priest,[6] notes that often in the treatment of religious obsessions, "What you really have to do is to help people straighten out their theology." In some cases, it is extremely helpful for a person's minister or priest is to be in regular contact with the OCD therapist. They can plan therapy conjointly, and both can learn from the experience.

Taking medications. If cognitive-behavioral therapy does not result in a noticeable improvement in OCD within two to three months, or if symptoms are so severe as to cause major interference in one's life, I strongly urge the use of medications. The majority of my patients with moderate to severe OCD take them and benefit. It should be kept in mind that OCD is associated with a unique chemical abnormality in the brain that responds specifically to the serotonin reuptake inhibitors, a group of medications that are safe and non-habit-forming.

I often spend a considerable amount of time trying to convince patients to take medications. Sometimes I remind them of this well-worn story: A man is driven to his rooftop by a flood. The water is rising quickly, and he prays desperately for a miracle. Three times, people come by in a boat and offer to pick him up. "No," he says, I have faith that God will save me." The man drowns and goes to heaven, where he asks God, "Why didn't you save me?" God answers, "I came by three times in a boat!" In the case of OCD, perhaps it is God who has provided medications. Maybe he wants you to use them.

Fortunately, it is not nearly as difficult to find a competent physician to prescribe medication for obsessive-compulsive disorder as it is to find a cognitive-behavioral therapist. Most psychiatrists today are well trained in the pharmacological treatment of OCD. In milder cases of the disorder, seeing one's family physician can work out well. A number of books, including my own previous text on OCD, describe in detail the pros and cons of the use of medications.

What It Takes to Have Trust: Three Christian Truths

It should be remembered that the psychological perspective—"If only I can transfer responsibility to God I can get better"—is not in the final analysis what is most important in the therapy developed by Luther, Bunyan, and Thérèse. After all, these premodern thinkers didn't know anything about our recent understanding of the cause and treatment of obsessions. What cured them was coming to a full awareness of the truth about God and themselves. They discovered a powerful dynamic that involves the convergence of three fundamental Christian truths: the helplessness of oneself, the power of God, and the mercy of God to those who confidently turn to him.[7]

Man's helplessness. Perhaps nothing is the equal of obsessive-compulsive disorder in producing a sense of personal helplessness. The disorder is within oneself, yet all attempts to overcome it appear only to make it worse. As we have observed before, Luther writes that in the monastery his fears drove him "to despair."[8] He "could not find peace, but was constantly crucified by thoughts."[9] Bunyan, during his relentless obsessional siege, was "tortured as if racked upon the wheel"[10] and driven to his "wits end."[11] Thérèse confided to her sister, "If only you knew

173

the darkness I am plunged into! Everything has disappeared on me.[12] . . . This trial is impossible to comprehend."[13]

Yet these three Christian greats all eventually came to see the necessity of their having been brought to their knees by their torment. Thérèse wrote near the end of her life, "The Almighty has done great things in the soul of His divine Mother's child, and the greatest thing is to have shown her littleness, her impotence."[14] Bunyan, in the last book that he wrote, *The Acceptable Sacrifice,* points out the need of a Christian being "broken hearted."[15]

In the normal, secular practice of psychotherapy, counselors teach people to fight against helplessness. They "empower" people with techniques for dealing with situations, thoughts, or moods. But for Christians, helplessness is actually desirable. It is an essential element in the therapy of trust, because one must feel helpless in order to fully turn to God. OCD sufferers, it seems, are a stubborn bunch. They have a special need to feel in control. God in his wisdom makes use of obsessions and compulsions to educate them on their powerlessness. Take heart, OCD sufferers, because your feeling of helplessness is your friend!

God's power. Luther, Bunyan, and Thérèse shared a classic view of God's omnipotence: God controls, arranges, and directs everything that happens in the universe. Luther, for example, writes, "The power of God is uncircumscribed and immeasurable, beyond and above all that is or may be."[16]

In the present day, God is often regarded as either a distant watchmaker who set the world running and then took leave, or as a comforting presence who exercises minimal control over the world's events. For the therapy of trust to work, however, God must be appreciated as he who is described in the Bible, in personal terms, a loving deity who can and does intervene in the world to take care of us and protect us from our fears.

The mercy of God. It was the final piece of the puzzle—a vivid recognition of the goodness of God to those who turn to him—that at last released Luther, Bunyan, and Thérèse from their terrifying struggles. They had become convinced of their helplessness, and they never doubted God's power. What allowed them to at last experience life-changing faith was a full appreciation of God's mercy.

During Luther's first decade in the monastery, he had seen God as a remote and punishing figure. After he discovered the true meaning of Romans 1:17, he suddenly underwent a revolution in his thought. "This is to behold God," he wrote, "that you should look upon his fatherly, friendly heart, in which there is no anger nor ungraciousness."[17] Bunyan's mystical experience, similarly, opened wide a door to God's love. He discovered a God who cared for him personally. "Now I could look from myself to him."[18] Thérèse describes her Little Way as a path of all of trust and love. It is giving oneself, "like a child, into the arms of the good God."[19]

Today, it seems that most Christians do not have a problem thinking of God as merciful. Psychologists tell us we live in a narcissistic age, in which people believe they are entitled to good things. Luther, Bunyan, and Thérèse would not agree. They understood that God's mercy is shown only to those who trust in him; and such trust, they knew, was not easy.

Why Bother with the Therapy of Trust?

It is not unreasonable for a Christian suffering from obsessive-compulsive disorder to forgo the approach described in this book, and to stick to standard treatments. The therapy of trust, after all, is relatively unknown and unproven, while cognitive-behavioral therapy and medications are established treatments that work very well.

For the committed Christian, however, OCD represents a rare opportunity for spiritual growth. Looking back on their lives, Luther, Bunyan, and Thérèse all remarked that they were glad they had suffered their tormenting fears, because through them they had learned invaluable lessons. Luther, for instance, said that without his severe trials he would not have been able "to understand Scripture, faith, the fear or the love of God" or "the meaning of hope."[20]

The therapy of trust, furthermore, provides a direct way for us to please God. Thérèse put this clearly. By the end of her life, she had no interest other than glorifying God through her trust in him. "What pleases God," she writes in a letter to her sister, "is the blind hope that I have in his mercy."[21]

Keep in mind that Martin Luther, John Bunyan, and Thérèse of Lisieux are truly Christian giants. No one would argue about Luther's being one of the greatest of all Christian thinkers. Bunyan, much less well known in the present day, may actually have influenced almost as many people. His *The Pilgrim's Progress* is said to be after the Bible the most published Christian book. Thérèse of Lisieux is not only the most popular Catholic saint of modern times, she is among a small group of individuals who have been declared "doctors" of the Catholic church for their distinguished theological contributions. The fact is that Luther, Bunyan, and Thérèse would be included on any thoughtful list of the dozen most influential and respected Christians of the last millennium, perhaps even of all time.

That all three suffered from obsessive-compulsive disorder and then found the same cure is extraordinary—and for the Christian with OCD it is surely providential. Can one afford to forgo their advice?

Epilogue

How Obsessive-Compulsive Disorder Saved Christianity

Luther's *sola fide* has been summed up by Paul Tillich, the twentieth century's most illustrious Lutheran theologian, as the "turning point" in Christian history when "a purified Christianity was able to establish itself." Luther's Reformation, according to Tillich, entailed a return to the vital message of the early Christians where "the relation to God is personal . . . an I-thou relationship mediated not by anybody or anything."[1] The recent "Joint Declaration of Faith" between Lutherans and Catholics recognizes Luther's contribution in bringing Catholic Christians, as well, back to a more Bible-based relationship with God. John Dillenberger, past president of the Graduate Theological Union in Berkeley, offers an assessment of Luther's monumental contribution to the Christian faith that would be agreed on by Christian theologians of all persuasions:

> The medieval church defined the righteousness of God as the demanding justice of God; for the mature Luther, by contrast, the righteousness of God was fundamentally the mercy of God.

Luther's great contribution centers in the recovery of the Biblical meaning of the righteousness of God.[2]

Bunyan's theological influence was similarly vast. His great accomplishment was to translate the theological insights of the Reformation into terms that were simple enough to be understood by the average person. As noted by Lord Macaulay, nineteenth-century English historian, *"The Pilgrim's Progress is the delight of the peasantry . . . loved by those who are too simple to admire it."*[3] Bunyan put *sola fide* in the form of a folk tale. Bunyan's legacy is that he too brought Christians back to the root of their faith.

A Dominican theologian writes of Thérèse of Lisieux, "We had to wait for Thérèse to rediscover a movement of spirituality which had all the fullness to fit exactly the dimensions of the Gospel."[4] John Paul II, the twentieth century's longest serving pope, and a noted theologian himself, observes, "Therese [revealed] to the men and women of our day the fundamental reality of the Gospel: the fact that we have really received a 'spirit of adoption' which makes us cry out: Abba! Father!"[5]

The theological significance of Luther, Bunyan, and Thérèse to the Christian church rests squarely on the fact that they brought Christians back to what may be considered the most cherished of biblical truths: the necessity of relying completely on God's goodness and mercy, as a child would trust blindly in a loving parent. In curing their obsessive-compulsive disorder, Luther, Bunyan, and Thérèse found anew the most essential part of the Christian faith.

In pursuing further the connection between obsessive-compulsive disorder and this "fundamental reality of the Gospel," it is enlightening to consider an analysis put forward by the great twentieth-century Jewish theologian Martin Buber. In a seminal book, *Two Types of Faith,* Buber begins with this proposition:

There are two, and only two, types of faith: The one from the fact that I trust someone . . . the other from the fact that I acknowledge a thing to be true.[6]

Religious faith, according to Buber, always involves, most basically, either trusting in God or believing in a revealed truth. It is the first type of faith, he suggests, that represents the heart of Judeo-Christian belief, and is displayed on every page of the Old Testament, as well as in every sermon by Jesus. It involves unconditional trust in a God who is personal, vital, loving, and trustworthy.

The second form of faith, Buber notes, was introduced into both Judaism and Christianity at a later date. In the case of Christianity it has often held sway, whether in the medieval church's emphasis on believing that a priest has forgiven one's sins or in the present-day evangelical churches' reliance on believing that one has been saved as a result of an altar call. What can be lost in this second form is the immediacy between God and man.

Buber's insightful distinction between the two different types of faith has a special relevance to obsessive-compulsive disorder. Throughout this book, the reader has been reminded that one of the most obvious and puzzling aspects of OCD is the inability of its sufferers to be reassured about their obsessional fears. People with religious obsessions can be told again and again that Jesus died for them, and that salvation awaits them, yet they still have agonizing doubts. Obsessionals, in fact, have great difficulty in believing in any fact that directly opposes one of their obsessions. OCD sufferers cannot even take as a fact what they see with their own eyes: they can stare straight at a light switch, see that it is off, and yet fear that it is on. Therefore, they must search for something stronger to overcome a tormenting fear. That something stronger can be trust in another person.

179

In her excellent biography *The Inner Life of Thérèse of Lisieux*, Patricia O'Connor takes note of the way that Buber's two types of faith battled for supremacy in the mind of Saint Thérèse. Catholicism of the nineteenth century, O'Connor states, was dominated by the type of faith that represents intellectual assent to a series of facts. While Thérèse never downplayed the importance of such faith, the normal creeds and rituals of the Catholic church simply could not quell her tormenting anxieties. Ultimately, Thérèse was able to make the critical distinction between believing that she was saved and trusting in God. O'Connor notes,

> While unable to believe without question that she would soon live with her Spouse forever, she continued to have confidence in God. . . . In her powerful trust, Thérèse never succumbed, despite the doubts, despite the darkness.[7]

Luther, Bunyan, and Thérèse all heroically found a unique and powerful form of therapy for obsessive-compulsive disorder. It rests on the pillar of truth that is repeatedly emphasized in both the Old Testament and in the Gospels: All that is needed is unconditional trust in God. What happens, unfortunately, is that in the Christian church this truth keeps on getting overshadowed by others. When this has happened, it has taken obsessive-compulsive disorder sufferers—theological canaries who can sense when individual responsibility has become choking—to take Christianity back to its pure source.

This question is offered for the reader's consideration: If Luther, Bunyan, and Thérèse can each and all be credited with bringing the Christian faith back to its most crucial theme— heartfelt trust in God and his mercy—and if it was obsessive-compulsive disorder that prodded them to this feat, then can it not be argued, with only slight exaggeration, that obsessive-compulsive disorder may have "saved" Christianity?

DSM-IV Diagnostic Criteria for Obsessive- Compulsive Disorder

The *Diagnostic and Statistical Manual of Mental Disorders*, published by the American Psychiatric Association, is the standard guide for diagnosing mental disorders in the United States and Canada. It is currently in its fourth edition, the "DSM-IV." Within the next five years a newer edition, the "DSM-V," should be published.

The DSM is a research-based, evolving document. A disorder is included in the manual only if strong evidence indicates that it is an independent syndrome that remains stable over time and is reliably diagnosed (i.e., the same individual will be diagnosed with the same disorder by different psychiatrists). Sometimes new disorders are added, and old ones deleted on the basis of new findings. Likewise, the diagnostic criteria for various disorders are adjusted on the basis of new data. In the case of OCD, an important recent change was the recognition of mental compulsions. Prior to the DSM-IV, compulsions were defined simply as behavioral, or observable, acts; now it is recognized that mental acts, or "thought compulsions," are also very common. The next major change in the DSM, some experts think, may be requiring that both obsessions and compulsions be present in order to make the diagnosis.

Psychiatric diagnosis, it must be remembered, remains at a relatively primitive stage compared to the rest of medicine. It is generally agreed that there are three levels of diagnostic sophistication. The first stands on the recognition of specific symptoms ("pneumonia is a cough with a fever"). The second level founds diagnosis on measurable biochemical changes in the body ("pneumonia is congestion in the lungs"). The third, the highest level of diagnostic refinement, fixes diagnosis firmly on the ultimate cause of a disorder ("pneumonia is a bacterial infection of the lungs"). While the other branches of medicine have advanced to levels two and three, psychiatry, for the most part, remains in the first stage, basing diagnosis purely on the basis of symptoms.

Obsessive-compulsive disorder, at this point in time, continues to be diagnosed completely on the basis of the recognition of its two cardinal symptoms, obsessions and compulsions. The DSM-IV starts off with a helpful overview:

> Obsessions are persistent ideas, thoughts, impulses or images that are experienced as intrusive and inappropriate and that cause marked anxiety or distress. The intrusive and inappropriate quality of the obsessions has been referred to as "ego-dystonic." This refers to the individual's sense that the content of the obsession is alien, not within his or her own control, and not the kind of thought that he or she would expect to have. However, the individual is able to recognize that the obsessions are the product of his or her own mind and are not imposed from without.
>
> Compulsions are repetitive behaviors (e.g., hand washing, ordering, checking) or mental acts (e.g., praying, counting, repeating words silently) the goal of which is to prevent or reduce anxiety or distress, not to provide pleasure or gratification. In most cases, the person feels driven to perform the compulsion to reduce the distress that accompanies an obsession or to prevent some dreaded event or situation.

The essential features of obsessive-compulsive disorder are recurrent obsessions or compulsions (Criterion A) that are severe enough to be time consuming (i.e., they take more than 1 hour per day) or cause marked distress or significant impairment (Criterion C). At some point during the course of the disorder, the person has recognized that the obsessions or compulsions are excessive or unreasonable (Criterion B). If another Axis 1 disorder is present, the content of the obsessions or compulsions is not restricted to it (Criterion D). The disturbance is not due to the direct physiological effects of a substance (e.g., a drug of abuse, a medication) or a general medical condition (Criterion E).

The official diagnostic criteria for OCD are as follows:
Obsessive-compulsive disorder is diagnosed when criteria A, B, C, D, and E are present:

A. Either obsessions or compulsions:
   Obsessions as defined by (1), (2), (3), and (4)
   (1) recurrent and persistent thoughts, impulses, or images that are experienced, at some time during the disturbance, as intrusive and inappropriate and that cause marked anxiety or distress
   (2) the thoughts, impulses, or images are not simply excessive worries about real-life problems
   (3) the person attempts to ignore or suppress such thoughts, impulses, or images, or to neutralize them with some other thought or action
   (4) the person recognizes that the obsessional thoughts, impulses, or images are a product of his or her own mind (not imposed from without as in thought insertion)

   Compulsions as defined by (1) and (2)
   (1) repetitive behaviors (e.g., hand washing, ordering, checking) or mental acts (e.g., praying, counting, repeating words silently) that the person feels driven to

perform in response to an obsession, or according to rules that must be applied rigidly

(2) the behaviors or mental acts are aimed at preventing or reducing distress or preventing some dreaded event or situation; however, these behaviors or mental acts either are not connected in a realistic way with what they are designed to neutralize or prevent or are clearly excessive

B. At some point during the course of the disorder, the person has recognized that the obsessions or compulsions are excessive or unreasonable. Note: This does not apply to children.

C. The obsessions or compulsions cause marked distress, are time consuming (take more than 1 hour a day), or significantly interfere with the person's normal routine, occupational (or academic) functioning, or usual social activities or relationships.

D. If another Axis 1 disorder is present, the content of the obsessions or compulsions is not restricted to it (e.g., preoccupation with food in the presence of Eating Disorder; hair pulling in the presence of Trichotillomania; concern with appearance in the presence of Body Dysmorphic Disorder; preoccupation with drugs in the presence of a Substance Use Disorder; preoccupation with having a serious illness in the presence of Hypochondriasis; preoccupation with sexual urges or fantasies in the presence of a Paraphilia; or guilty ruminations in the presence of Major Depressive Disorder).

E. The disturbance is not due to the direct physiological effects of a substance (e.g., a drug of abuse, a medication) or a general medical condition.

The Yale-Brown Obsessive Compulsive Scale

The Yale-Brown Obsessive Compulsive Scale (Y-BOCS), developed in 1989 by Yale and Brown Universities, is the most widely used of OCD scales in the United States. Its strong point is its simplicity and ease of use. Asking just ten questions, it provides a general measure of the strength of a person's obsessions and compulsions. Its only drawback is its inadequate measurement of avoidance. If avoidance is a major problem (e.g., you never enter your kitchen because of contamination obsessions), your OCD is likely somewhat worse than the test suggests.

The Y-BOCS consists of five questions about obsessions and five very similar inquiries regarding compulsions. Each item is given a rating of 0 to 4, the total score for the test being the sum of the ratings for all ten. Usually, a score of 0 to 7 is within the normal range; 8 to 15 indicates mild OCD; 16 to 25, moderate OCD; and 26 and above, severe OCD. Most people who present for treatment of OCD have scores in the 20 to 25 range. Studies suggest that 2 percent of the population will score 18 or above.

Instructions: Read and answer the following questions. Don't spend too much time trying to decide—just check the answer that seems to fit best.

1. How much of your time is occupied by obsessive thoughts? How frequently do the obsessive thoughts occur?
   0 = None.
   1 = Less than 1 hour per day, or occasional intrusions (occur not more than 8 times a day).
   2 = 1 to 3 hours per day, or frequent intrusions (occur more than 8 times a day, but most hours of the day are free of obsessions).
   3 = More than 3 and up to 8 hours per day, or very frequent intrusions.
   4 = More than 8 hours per day, or near-constant intrusions.

2. How much do your obsessive thoughts interfere with your work, school, social, or other important role functioning? Is there anything you don't do because of them?
   0 = None.
   1 = Slight interference with social or other activities, but overall performance not impaired.
   2 = Definite interference with social or occupational performance, but still manageable.
   3 = Causes substantial impairment in social or occupational performance.
   4 = Incapacitating.

3. How much distress do your obsessions cause you?
   0 = None.
   1 = Not too disturbing.
   2 = Disturbing but still manageable.

186

3 = Very disturbing.

4 = Near-constant and disabling distress.

4. How much of an effort do you make to resist the obsessive thoughts? How often do you try to turn your attention away from these thoughts as they enter your mind?

   0 = Try to resist all the time (or the symptoms are so minimal that there is no need to actively resist them).

   1 = Try to resist most of the time.

   2 = Make some effort to resist.

   3 = Yield to all obsessions without attempting to control them, but I do so with some reluctance.

   4 = Completely and willingly give in to all obsessions.

5. How much control do you have over your obsessive thoughts? How successful are you in stopping or diverting your obsessive thinking? (Note: do not include here obsessions stopped by doing compulsions.)

   0 = Complete control.

   1 = Usually able to stop or divert obsessions with some effort and concentration.

   2 = Sometimes able to stop or divert obsessions.

   3 = Rarely successful in stopping obsessions, can only divert attention with difficulty.

   4 = Obsessions are completely involuntary, rarely able to even momentarily alter obsessive thinking.

6. How much time do you spend performing compulsive behaviors? How much longer than most people does it take to complete routine activities because of your rituals? How frequently do you perform rituals?

   0 = None.

   1 = Less than 1 hour per day, or occasional performance of compulsive behaviors (no more than 8 times a day).

2 = From 1 to 3 hours per day, or frequent performance of compulsive behaviors (more than 8 times a day, but most hours are free of compulsions).

3 = More than 3 and up to 8 hours per day, or very frequent performance of compulsive behaviors.

4 = More than 8 hours per day, or near constant performance of compulsive behaviors.

7. How much do your compulsive behaviors interfere with your work, school, social, or other important role functioning? Is there anything that you don't do because of the compulsions?

0 = None.

1 = Slight interference with social or other activities, but overall performance not impaired.

2 = Definite interference with social or occupational performance, but still manageable.

3 = Causes substantial impairment in social or occupational performance.

4 = Incapacitating.

8. How would you feel if prevented from performing your compulsions(s)? How anxious would you become?

0 = None.

1 = Only slightly anxious if compulsions prevented.

2 = Anxiety would mount but remain manageable if compulsions prevented.

3 = Prominent and very disturbing increase in anxiety if compulsions interrupted.

4 = Incapacitating anxiety from any intervention aimed at modifying activity.

9. How much of an effort do you make to resist the compulsions?

0 = Always try to resist (or the symptoms are so minimal that there is no need to actively resist them).

1 = Try to resist most of the time.

2 = Make some effort to resist.

3 = Yield to almost all compulsions without attempting to control them, but with some reluctance.

4 = Completely and willingly yield to all compulsions.

10. How strong is the drive to perform the compulsive behavior? How much control do you have over the compulsions?

0 = Complete control.

1 = Pressure to perform the behavior, but usually able to exercise voluntary control over it.

2 = Strong pressure to perform behavior, can control it only with difficulty.

3 = Very strong drive to perform behavior, must be carried to completion, can only delay with difficulty.

4 = Drive to perform behavior experienced as completely involuntary and overpowering, rarely able to even momentarily delay activity.

Notes

Prologue

1. C. Breitner, quoted in Edna Foa, "Behavioral Treatment of Obsessive-Compulsive Patients,' *Highland Highlights*, 13 no. 1, 25.

2. The Sisters of the Visitation, *The Spirit of Saint Jane de Chantal* (London: Longmans, Green, and Co., 1922), 2.

3. Richard Greaves, *John Bunyan* (Grand Rapids: Eerdmans, 1969), 156.

4. Hans Urs von Balthasar, *Two Sisters in the Spirit*, trans. Dennis Martin (San Francisco: Ignatius Press, 1970), 96.

5. William James, *The Varieties of Religious Experience* (Chicago: New American Library, 1958), 76.

Chapter 1: Introduction

1. Before Freud psychiatrists had been rather friendly towards religion. They had regarded it as a separate yet complementary approach to mental health. Amariah Brigham, for instance, first editor of the prestigious *American Journal of Psychiatry*, had written only a decade before Freud came to prominence that psychiatric treatment should be based on "religious instruction and medical advice."

2. Sigmund Freud, *The Future of an Illusion* (New York: W. W. Norton & Company, 1989), 56.

3. O. Fenichel, quoted in *Psychiatric Annals*, August 2000, 552. Otto Fenichel was a highly respected mid-twentieth-century psychoanalyst. Full quote: "It has been said that religious people in analysis remain uninfluenced in their religious philosophies. I consider this not to be correct. Repeatedly I have seen that with the analysis of the sexual anxieties and with the maturing of the personality, the attachment to religion has ended."

4. Albert Ellis, *Case Against Religiosity* (New York: Institute for Rational Emotive Therapy, 1983), 1.

5. In 1983 a long-term study of alcoholics by esteemed Harvard researcher George Vaillant disclosed that the single most important factor in recovery from alcoholism is regular attendance at AA meetings. G. E. Vaillant, *The Natural History of Alcoholism* (Cambridge, MA: Harvard University Press, 1983).

In the 1990s "Project MATCH," one of the largest studies of psychotherapy ever undertaken, studied 1,746 alcohol-dependent patients from ten different sites. Patients were randomly assigned to receive three different treatments—cognitive-behavioral therapy, motivational-enhancement therapy, and 12–step facilitation therapy—based on AA. All three therapies worked; the only significant difference between them was that the AA-based program was associated with more abstinence at a one year follow-up. M. Miller, *The Psychiatric Clinics of North America* (Philadelphia: W. B. Saunders: June 1999), 431.

6. In a representative study, psychiatrist Harold Koenig of Duke University followed eighty-seven severely depressed patients over the course of a year and found that their degree of "intrinsic religiosity" (how important personal religious beliefs are to an individual) predicted remission. H.G. Koenig, "Religiosity and Remission of Depression in Medically Ill Older Patients," *American Journal of Psychiatry* 155, no. 4 (1998): 536–42.

Psychiatrist David Larson, president of National Institute for Healthcare Research, cautiously summarized the results of studies in the October 1998 issue of *Clinical Psychiatry News*: "The evidence to date suggest merely that there is an association between increased religiousness or spirituality and better physical and mental health. . . . The associations have been relatively moderate in magnitude," 43.

For reviews of the apparently therapeutic role of religious belief in mental and physical disorders, see books and articles by Harold Koenig, David Larson, and Len Sperry. The journal *Psychiatric Annals* reviewed the topic "spirituality and clinical practice" in its August 2000 and March 2006 issues. It must also be kept in mind, however, that there are numerous case reports of individual psychopathology associated with a rigid religious upbringing and cults.

7. Pascal Boyer, *Religion Explained* (New York: Basic Books, 2001).

8. *Psychiatric Annals*, August 2000, 529.

9. Freud, *Future of an Illusion*, 55. Freud goes on to state that believing in religion is akin to "a state of blissful hallucinatory confusion."

10. J. L. Rapoport, A. Swedo, H. Leonard, "Obsessive-Compulsive Disorder," in *Child and Adolescent Psychiatry: Modern Approaches*, 3rd ed., M. Rutter, E. Taylor, L. Hersov, (Oxford: Blackwell Science, 1995).

11. Karl Westphal, quoted in Roger Pitman, "Obsessive-Compulsive Disorder in Western History," in *Current Insights in Obsessive-Compulsive Disorder*, ed. E. Hollander, J. Zohar, D. Marazzti, and B. Olivier (Chichester, England: John Wiley and Sons, 1994).

12. Aubrey Lewis, "Problems of Obsessional Illness," *Proceedings of the Royal Society of Medicine*, December 10, 1935, 325.

13. "The Epidemiological Catchment Area Study." A recent book summarizing this important study is L. N. Robbins and D. A. Regier, eds., *Psychiatric Disorder in America* (New York: Free Press, 1991).

Chapter 2: Renaissance Anxieties

1. J. Basil Oldham, *The Renaissance* (London: J. M. Dent and Sons, 1912).

2. Jacob B. Burckhardt, *The Civilization of the Renaissance in Italy* (1860), Burckhardt quoted in Roy Porter, *Rewriting the Self* (London: Routledge, 1997), 17. He was a Swiss cultural historian, perhaps the most famous writer on the Renaissance.

3. Agnes Heller, *Renaissance Man* (London: Routledge and Kegan Paul, 1967).

4. *New York Times Magazine*, "The Me Millennium," October 17, 1999.

5. Thomas Tentler, *Sin and Confession on the Eve of the Reformation* (Princeton, NJ: Princeton University Press, 1977), 134.

6. John Mahoney, *The Making of Moral Theology* (Oxford: Clarendon Press, 1987), 27.

7. Ladislav Orsy, *The Evolving Church and the Sacrament of Penance* (Denville, NJ: Dimension Books, 1982), 128.

8. Gregory Zilboorg, *A History of Medical Psychology* (New York: Norton, 1941), 133.

9. Rudolph M. Bell, *Holy Anorexia* (Chicago: University of Chicago Press, 1985).

10. John Donne, quoted in Lawrence Babb, *Elizabethan Malady* (East Lansing, MI: Michigan State College Press, 1951), 185.

11. See the discussion in chap. 6 on culture and OCD.

12. Tentler, *Sin and Confession*, 91.

13. William of Auvergne, quoted in Peter Biller and A. J. Minnis, eds., *Handling Sin: Confession in the Middle Ages* (Rochester, NY: York Medieval Press, 1998), 96, quoted in essay by Lesley Smith, "William Auvergne and Confession."

14. Tentler, *Sin and Confession*, 103.

15. Ignatius of Loyola, *Saint Ignatius' Own Story: As Told to Luis Gonzales de Camara*, trans. William J. Young (Chicago: Loyola University Press, 1980), 19. (Ignatius used the third person to describe himself. I have taken the liberty of putting his words into the first person.) Ignatius reluctantly dictated his autobiography at the end of his life after receiving much pressure to do so from his followers. Candido de Dalmases observes that "Ignatius developed an anguishing and prolonged combat with scruples. He was besieged by doubts of having omitted some sin, or of not having sufficiently explained those he had confessed." Candido de Dalmases, *Ignatius of Loyola: Founder of the Jesuits* (Saint Louis: Institute of Jesuit Resources, 1985), 58.

16. Ignatius, *Saint Ignatius' Own Story*, 20.

17. Ignatius, *The Spiritual Exercises of Saint Ignatius*, trans. by Louis J. Puhl, SJ (Chicago: Loyola University Press, 1951), 154.

18. John Baptist Scaramelli, SJ, *The Directorium Asceticum* (London: Burns, Oates and Washbourne, 1924), 325.

19. Thomas à Kempis, *The Imitation of Christ*, www.leaderu.com/cyber/books/imitation/foreword.html), bk. 3, chap. 6.

20. The Sisters of the Visitation, *The Spirit of Saint Jane de Chantal as Shown by Her Letters* (New York: Longmans, Green, and Co., 1922), 2 and 5.

21. Jean Gerson, quoted in Tentler, *Sin and Confession*, 77.

22. Antoninus of Florence, *Confessionale—Defecerunt*, 8, quoted in Tentler, *Sin and Confession*, 77.

23. Gerson, quoted in Tentler, *Sin and Confession*, 77.

24. Johannes von Dambach, quoted in Tentler, *Sin and Confession*, 114.

25. Ibid., 114.

26. See Roland Bainton, *Here I Stand: A Life of Martin Luther* (New York: Meridian Publishers, 1995), 24.

27. Richard Hunter and Ida MacAlpine, *Three Hundred Years of Psychiatry* (Hartsdale, NY: Carlisle Publishing, 1982), 33.

28. Michael MacDonald, *Mystical Bedlam* (Cambridge: Cambridge University Press, 1984), 200.

Chapter 3: Martin Luther

1. Ralph Waldo Emerson, quoted in Peter Manns, *Martin Luther* (New York: Cross-road, 1911, repr., 1983), 6.

2. Preserved Smith, *The Life and Letters of Martin Luther* (1911; repr., New York: Barnes and Noble, 1968).

3. Johannes Cochlaeus, *Commentaria de actis et scriptis Martin: Lutheri* (Mainz, 1549).

4. Pietro Vergerio, quoted in Heiko Oberman, *Luther: Man Between God and the Devil* (New York: Image Books, 1992), 88.

5. Ignaz von Döllinger, quoted in Eric Gritsch, *Martin—God's Court Jester* (Philadelphia: Fortress, 1983), 204.

6. Hartmann Grisar, quoted in Gritsch, *Martin*, 205

7. Paul Reiter, quoted in Erik H. Erikson, *Young Man Luther* (New York: Norton, 1958), 27.

8. Erikson, *Young Man Luther*, 148.

9. Roger Johnson, *Psychohistory and Religion: The Case of Young Martin Luther* (Philadelphia: Fortress, 1977), 8.

10. Most biographers classified Luther's psychological problems as either anxiety or depression, or both. The highly respected German historian Rudolf Thiel refers in his 1953 biography, *Luther*, to "attacks of nameless, monstrous anxiety." German scholar Richard Friedenthal in his 1967 *Luther: His Life and Times*, diagnoses "frequent attacks of severe depression, attacks of a psychopathic nature." Eric Gritsch, in an outstanding biography written in 1983, *Martin—God's Court Jester*, observes that "throughout his life Luther was subject to bouts of anxiety ranging from simple doubts to deep depressions." Richard Marius, in his 1999 *Martin Luther: The Christian between God and Death* (Cambridge, MA: Harvard University Press, 1999), the most detailed psychological study of Luther since Erik Erikson's, concludes, "It seems probable that Luther's suffering arose from a disposition prone to melancholy—we would say depression, even 'clinical' depression of a sort that might require treatment." No one, it may be noted, suggests that Luther's main problem was obsessive-compulsive disorder.

11. Roland H. Bainton, *Here I Stand: A Life of Martin Luther* (New York: Meridian, 1995), 42.

12. Ibid., 20. Bainton writes that Luther suffered depression for six months prior to his entrance into the monastery.

13. Luther, quoted in Marius, *Martin Luther*, 44.

14. Martin Luther, *Luther's Works*, ed. Jaroslav Pelikan and Helmut T. Lehmann (Philadelphia: Concordia and Fortress, 1976), vol. 31 ("Explanations of the Ninety-Five Theses"), 129.

15. Luther, *Luther's Works*, vol. 27 ("Galatians"), 73.

16. Luther, *Luther's Works*, vol. 34 ("Latin Writings"), 336.

17. Luther, *Luther's Works*, vol. 27 ("Galatians"), 13.

18. Bainton, *Here I Stand*, 41.

19. Luther, *Luther's Works*, vol. 48 ("Letters"), 333.

20. Bainton, *Here I Stand*, 284.

21. The reference to painful pictures of a knife, suggesting violent harm obsessions, was found in a source that could be considered questionable: Father de Lehen, SJ, *The Way of Interior Peace* (Chicago: Benziger Brothers, 1889), 340.

22. Marius, *Martin Luther*, 214.

23. Luther, *Luther's Works*, vol. 27 ("Galatians"), 73.

24. Luther, *Luther's Works*, vol. 14 ("Psalms"), 84.

25. Luther, *Luther's Works*, vol. 54 ("Table Talk"), 93.

26. Luther, *Luther's Works*, vol. 14 ("Psalms"), 37.

27. Luther, *Luther's Works*, vol. 54 ("Table Talk"), 194.

28. From Luther's song, "Rejoice Together, Beloved Christians," surely an autobiographical reference. Quoted as such in Oberman, *Luther*, 319.

29. Luther, *Luther's Works*, vol. 5 ("Genesis"), 157.

30. Luther, *Luther's Works*, vol. 54 ("Table Talk"), 94.

31. Obstruction of confession . . . this is Fellow monk of Luther's quoted in Erikson, 156. The veracity of the story is not certain.

32. only truly afflicted . . . Luther, *Luther's Works*, vol 54 ("Table Talk"), 339.

33. my body was horribly . . . Luther, *Luther's Works*, vol 8 ("Genesis"), 173.

34. The frost alone . . . Luther, *Luther's Works*, vol 12 ("John"), 24.

35. prayers I mumbled . . . Luther, *Luther's Works*, vol 5 ("Genesis"), 271.

36. longer I tried to heal . . . Luther, *Luther's Works*, vol 27 ("Galatians"), 13.

37. would have killed myself . . . Luther, *Luther's Works*, vol 17 ("Isaiah"), 111.

38. taught to understand . . . Luther, *Luther's Works*, vol 34 ("Latin Writings"), 336.

39. Luther wrote, "God gives righteousness through His mercy." This is Luther's key insight. Two of his clearest explanations regarding how he came to the insight are the following:

"At last, by the mercy of God, meditating day and night, I gave heed to the context of the words . . . 'He who through faith is righteous shall live.' There I began to understand that the righteousness of God is that by which the righteous [person] lives by a gift of God, namely by faith." *Luther's Works*, vol. 34 ("Latin Writings"), 377.

"When by God's grace I pondered over the words, 'He who through faith is righteous shall live' (Rom. 1:17), I soon came to the conclusion that if we, who are righteous men, ought to live from faith and if the righteousness of God should contribute to the salvation of all who believe, then salvation won't be on our merit but God's mercy." *Luther's Works*, vol. 54 ("Table Talk"), 193.

40. Bainton, *Here I Stand*, 50.

41. Luther, *Luther's Works*, vol. 34 ("Latin Writings"), 337.

42. Bainton, *Here I Stand*, 87.

43. Luther, *Luther's Works*, vol. 1 ("Genesis"), 287.

44. Luther, *Luther's Works*, vol. 12 ("Psalms"), 315.

45. Luther, *Luther's Works*, vol. 8 ("Genesis"), 173.

46. Luther, *Luther's Works*, vol. 5 ("Genesis), 271; and *Luther's Works*, vol. 28 ("First Corinthians"), 81.

47. Luther, *Luther's Works*, vol. 54 ("Table Talk"), 94.

48. Sigmond Freud, quoted in Judith Rapoport, *The Boy Who Couldn't Stop Washing* (New York: Dutton, 1989), 12.

49. Marius, *Martin Luther*, xiii.

50. Luther, *Luther's Works*, vol. 1 ("Genesis"), 287.

51. Bainton, *Here I Stand*, 127.

Chapter 4: John Bunyan

1. Jeremy Taylor, *The Whole Works of the Right Rev. Jeremy Taylor, D.D.*, vol. XII, "The Rule of Conscience" (London: C. and J. Rivington, 1828), 172–76.

2. Kathleen Swaim, *Pilgrim's Progress, Puritan Progress* (Chicago: University of Illinois Press, 1993), 8.

3. Richard Baxter, *The Christian Directory*, chapter on "Symptoms of Melancholy," 263.

4. James, *Varieties of Religious Experience*, 133.

5. Peter Bowden, quoted in Christopher Hill, *A Tinker and a Poor Man* (New York: Norton, paperback, 1988), 16.

6. John Bunyan, *Grace Abounding to the Chief of Sinners* (New York: Viking Penguin, 1987), 8.

7. G. B. Harrison, *John Bunyan. A Study in Personality* (New York: Doubleday, 1928), 17.

8. Bunyan, *Grace Abounding*, 8.

9. W. Hale White, *John Bunyan*, quoted by F. Renaissance Leavis in afterword to *The Pilgrim's Progress* (New York: New American Library, 1981), 287.

10. W. R.Owens, introduction to *Grace Abounding*, xxii.

11. Bunyan, *Grace Abounding*, 47.

12. Ibid., 11.

13. Ibid., 13.

14. Ibid., 27.

15. Ibid., 19.

16. Ibid., 28.

17. Ibid., 27.

18. Hill, *Tinker and a Poor Man*, 73.

19. Bunyan, *Grace Abounding*, 43.

20. Ibid., 36.

21. Ibid., 36.

22. Ibid., 36.

23. Ibid., 36.

24. Ibid., 13.

25. Ibid., 28, 29.

26 Ibid., 23.

27 Ibid., 64.

28. Ibid., 42.

29. Ibid., 28.

30. Ibid., 46.

31. Ibid., 57.

32. Ibid., 54, 55.

33. Ibid., 41.

34. Ibid., 24.

35. Ibid., 24.

36. Ibid., 59.

37. Ibid., 59.

38. Ibid., 60.

39. Ibid., 67.

40. Ibid., 73.

41. Roger Sharrock, *John Bunyan* (New York: St. Martin's Press, 1968), 57.

42. Monica Furlong, *Puritan's Progress* (New York: Coward, McCann, and Geoghegan, 1975), 19.

43. Gordon Wakefield, *Bunyan the Christian* (London: HarperCollins, 1992), 16.

44. R. H. Thouless, quoted in Furlong, *Puritan's Progress* 157.

45. Ernst Bacon, *Pilgrim and a Dreamer: John Bunyan: His Life and Work* (Australia: Paternoster Press, 1983), 66.

46. See Furlong, *Puritan's Progress*, 157.

47. Furlong, *Puritan's Progress*, 211.

48. See the chapter in Sharrock's *John Bunyan* on the writing of *The Pilgrim's Progress*.

49. John Bunyan, *The Pilgrim's Progress* (New York: New American Library, paperback, 1981). On the title page Bunyan states that the book is written "in the similitude of a dream." In the foreword, or "apology," he advises that the book "will direct thee to the Holy Land."

50. Bunyan, *Pilgrim's Progress*, 27.

51. Ibid., 109.

52. Ibid., 143.

53. Ibid., 131.

54. Ibid., 144.

55. Harrison, *John Bunyan*, 3.

56. Thomas H. Luxon, *Literal Figures: Puritan Allegory and the Reformation Crisis in Representation* (Chicago: University of Chicago Press, 1995).

57. Bunyan, *Pilgrim's Progress*, 83.

58. Robert A. Roseo, *John Bunyan: God's Tinker* (Fort Washington, PA: CLC Press, 1999), 114.

59. Harrison, *John Bunyan*, 170.

Chapter 5: Saint Thérèse

1. Patricia O'Connor, *Thérèse of Lisieux: A Biography* (Huntington, IN: Our Sunday Visitor, 1983), 17.

2. This quotes and the preceding one are from a tape by Fr. Dolan (past director of the "Little Flower Society" in the USA): "Fr. Dolan Interviews the Sisters of St. Therese." These two quotes are from one of Thérèse's teachers at school.

3. St. Thérèse of Lisieux, *Story of a Soul: The Autobiography of St. Therese of Lisieux,* trans. by John Clark (Washington, DC: ICS Publications, 1972), 53.

4. Ibid., 58.

5. Letter from Pauline to Thérèse, December 20, 1882, *Letters of St. Therese of Lisieux*, vol. 1 (Washington, DC: ICS, 1972), 154.

6. Thérèse, *Story of a Soul*, 60.

7. Thérèse, 61.

8. Thérèse, 67.

9. Thérèse, 62.

10. Patricia O'Connor *The Inner Life of Therese of Lisieux* (Huntington, IN: Our Sunday Visitor, 1997), 110.

11. Thérèse, *Story of a Soul*, 84.

12. Christopher O'Mahoney, ed. and trans., *St. Therese of Lisieux by Those Who Knew Her* (Dublin: Veritas, 1975), 44.

13. Thérèse, *Story of a Soul*, pp. 84–85.

14. O'Mahony, *St. Therese*, 88.

15. Thérèse, *Story of a Soul*, 88.

16. Ibid., 97.

17. O'Connor, *Inner Life of Therese*, 34.

18. Janet, *Les Obsessions et la Psychiasthenie* (Paris: Alcan, 1903).

19. Thérèse, *Story of a Soul*, 252.

20. O'Mahony, *St. Therese*, 62, quoted by Pauline.

21. Thérèse, *Story of a Soul*, 149.

22. Ibid., 166.

23. Thérèse, *Letters*, vol. 1, 567. Therese's cousin, Marie Guerin, was almost like another sister to her. In several letters, and apparently also in private conversations, Marie told Thérèse about her agonies with "bad thoughts." We know OCD has a strong genetic component. See also letters on 638 and 1112 in vol. 2 of *Letters*.

24. Thérèse, *Story of a Soul*, 149.

25. A priest, *Letters*, vol. 1, 585; *Letters*, vol. 2, 767 (Fr. Pichon, Thérèse's first director).

26. *St. Therese of Lisieux: Her Last Conversations* (Washington, DC: ICS Publications, 1977), 58.

27. Sister Genevieve of the Holy Face, *My Sister Saint Therese* (Rockford, IL: Tan Books, 1959), 47.

28. Thérèse, *Last Conversations*, 129.

29. Thérèse, *Letters*, vol. 2, 796.

30. Thérèse, *Last Conversations*, 140.

31. Sub-prioress, quoted in Guy Gaucher, *The Story of a Life* (San Francisco: Harper, 1987), 126.

32. O'Mahony, *St. Therese of Lisieux*, 46, as recounted by Pauline.

33. Thérèse, *Story of a Soul*, 211.

34. Christopher O'Donnell, *Love in the Heart of the Church* (Dublin: Veritas, 1997), 171.

35. Thérèse, *Story of a Soul*, 211.

36. Thérèse, *Last Conversations*, 257.

37. Thérèse, *Story of a Soul*, 213.

38. O'Donnell, *Love in the Heart of the Church*, 173.

39. Thérèse, *Last Conversations*, 258.

40. Thérèse, quoted in Guy Gaucher, *The Passion of Therese of Lisieux* (New York: Crossroad, 1973), 115. Bishop Gaucher, widely considered Thérèse's most authoritative biographer, comments on "the acts of faith that she had to keep on making in the face of her continuing doubts."

41. Thérèse, *Story of a Soul*, 213.

42. Thérèse, *Last Conversations*, 140.

43. Thérèse, *Letters*, vol. 2, 999. From one of Thérèse's most powerful letters, written September, 17, 1896, to her sister Marie. In the context of an examination of her own motives and desires, Thérèse writes, "What pleases God is that He sees me loving my littleness and my poverty, the blind hope that I have in His mercy."

44. Thérèse, *Last Conversations*, 77.

45. Ibid., 62.

46. In his book *The Power of Confidence* (New York: Alba House, 1998), Conrad De Meester quotes a German authority who in 1955 called Thérèse "the saint of the obsessive neurotics" (xxxii). Generally, however, no biographer has recognized that Thérèse had what we now call obsessive-compulsive disorder. This is explained largely by the fact that only recently have the diagnostic criteria for the disorder been clarified sufficiently to make it obvious. Likewise, her biographers have missed the significance of her "strange illness."

47. Ida Görres, *The Hidden Face: A Study of St Therese of Lisieux* (New York: Pantheon, 1959) 78, 76.

48. Tape by Fr. Marc Foley, OCD, "St. Therese: Psychological and Spiritual Perspective on Her Childhood Illness."

49. Pope Pius XI, at the canonization Mass of Thérèse in 1925, declared that Thérèse's mission had been to reveal to us the path of "spiritual childhood" as a "sure way of salvation." Quoted in Francois Jamart, *Complete Spiritual Doctrine of Saint Therese* (New York: Saint Paul Publications, 1961), 24.

50. Thérèse, *Story of a Soul*, 15.

51. Ibid., 75.

52. Thérèse's mother, *Letters*, vol. 2, 1222–23.

53. Thérèse's mother, *Story of a Soul*, 28.

54. Ibid., 43.

55. O'Connor, *Inner Life of Therese*, 181.

56. Monica Furlong, *Therese of Lisieux* (New York: Pantheon, 1987), 27.

57. Thérèse, *Story of a Soul*, 34.

58. Thérèse's aunt, *Letters*, vol. 2, 131–35.

59. Thérèse, *Story of a Soul*, 49.

60. Ibid., 17 and 29.

Chapter 6: What Causes Obsessive-Compulsive Disorder?

1. Aubrey Lewis, MD, "Problems of Obsessional Illness," *Proceedings of the Royal Society of Medicine*, December 10, 1935, 325.

2. Well-known psychiatric researchers Donald Goodwin and Samuel Guze, authors of the authoritative text *Psychiatric Diagnosis*, reviewed the treatment of obsessive-compulsive disorder with psychoanalysis and related therapies, and concluded that there was no evidence at all to support their value, *Psychiatric Diagnosis* (New York: Oxford University Press, 1996), 145.

3. S. Rachman and De Silva, "Abnormal and Normal Obsessions," *Behavior Research and Therapy* 16 (1978): 233–48.

4. Christine Purdon and David Clark, "Obsessive Intrusive Thoughts in Nonclinical Subjects," *Behavior Research and Therapy* 31 (1993): 713–20.

5. S. Rachman, "Obsessions, Responsibility, and Guilt," *Behavior Research and Therapy* 31 (1993): 149–54.This excellent paper lays out very clearly the understanding of OCD that I am trying to get across.

6. See Wegner's interesting book that reviews this research: *White Bears and Other Unwanted Thoughts* (New York: Penguin, 1989).

7. Lecture in 1991 by Judith Rapoport, MD reviewed in "Psychiatric News," January 3, 1992, 6.

8. Paul Salkovskis, "Cognitive-Behavioural Factors and the Persistence of Intrusive Thoughts in Obsessional Problems." *Behavior Research and Therapy* 27 (1989): 677–84.

9. M. Salkovskis et al., "Responsibility Attitudes and Interpretations Are Characteristic of Obsessive-Compulsive Disorder," *Behavior Research and Therapy* 38 (2000): 347–72.

10. Roz Shafran, "The Manipulation of Responsibility in Obsessive-Compulsive Disorder," *British Journal of Clinical Psychology* 36 (1997): 397–407.

11. Edna Foa et al., "Inflated Perception of Responsibility for Harm in Obsessive-Compulsive Disorder," *Journal of Anxiety Disorders*, 15 (2001): 259–75.

12. A. Wroe and Salkovskis, "Causing Harm and Allowing Harm: A Study of Beliefs in Obsessional Problems," *Behavior Research and Therapy* 38 (2000): 1141–62. Also see Salkovskis et al., "Cognitive-Behavioural Approach to Understanding Obsessional Thinking," *British Journal of Psychiatry* 173 (1998): 53–63.

13. Stanley Rachman and Ray Hodgson, *Obsessions and Compulsions*, Century Psychology Series (Englewood Cliffs, NJ: Prentice Hall, 1980), 16.

14. Richard Hunter and Ida MacAlpine, *Three Hundred Years of Psychiatry* (Hartsdale, NY: Carlisle Publishing, 1982), 253.

15. Historian J. Jerome, writing in the French *Review La Vie Spiritelle*, observes that there is "no mention of scruples in the annals of Moral Theology, until the end of the Middle Ages." Quoted by Father Thomas Santa, a Liguorian priest and editor of the magazine *Scrupulous Anonymous*, on page 1 in the December 1998 issue. Also, Father Santa, an expert on the history of scruples, made this point himself in a personal communication to me.

16. Gerald Edelman and Giulio Tononi, *A Universe of Consciousness* (New York: Basic Books, 2000), 189.

17. Roger Pitman, chapter entitled "Historical Considerations" in Joseph Zohar, Thomas Insel, and Steven Rasmussen, *Psychobiology of Obsessive-Compulsive Disorder* (New York: Springer, 1991). Also see Roger Pitman, "A Cybernetic Model of Obsessive-Compulsive Psychopathology." *Comprehensive Psychiatry*, 28 (July 1987): 334–43.

18. O'Mahony, *St. Therese*, 184.

19. O'Mahony, *St. Therese*, 152.

20. Thérèse's cousin, quoted in Patricia O'Connor, *Therese of Lisieux* (Huntington, IN: Our Sunday Visitor Publications, 1983), 19.

21. *Story of a Soul, The Autobiography of St. Therese of Lisieux*, trans. John Clark (Washington, DC: ICS Publications, 1972), 62.

22. Thérèse's sister Marie, *Letters*, vol. 1, 162.

23. H. Houston Merritt, *Merritt's Textbook of Neurology*, 8th ed., ed., Lewis Rowland (Philadelphia: Lea & Febigee, 1989).

24. Susan E. Swedo, Judith L. Rapoport, et al., "High Prevalence of Obsessive-Compulsive Symptoms in Patients with Sydenham's Chorea," *American Journal of Psychiatry* 146 no. 2 (February, 1989): 246–49. Also see Susan E. Swedo et al., "The PANDAS Subgroup," *CNS Spectrums* 6 (May 2001): 419–25.

25. *Story of a Soul*, 44.

26. Ibid., 76.

27. Ibid., 44.

28. *Letters*, vol. 2 (Pauline writing to Celine).

Chapter 7: Treating Obsessive-Compulsive Disorder

1. V. Meyer, Renaissance Levy, and A. Schnurer, quoted in Gail Steketee, *Treatment of Obsessive-Compulsive Disorder* (New York: Guilford, 1993), 29.

2. Aaron Beck, A. Rush, Brian Shaw, and Gary Emery, *Cognitive Therapy of Depression* (New York: Guilford, 1979).

3. The "bible" of RET is Ellis's *Reason and Emotion in Psychotherapy* (Secaucus, NJ: Lyle Stuart, 1973).

4. Paul Emmelkamp and H. Beens, "Cognitive Therapy with Obsessive-Compulsive Disorder," *Behavior Research and Therapy* 29 (1991): 293–300.

5. The first of the studies employing Beck's model was: Patricia Van Oppen, et al., "Cognitive Therapy and Exposure in Vivo in the Treatment of Obsessive-Compulsive Disorder," *Behavior Research and Therapy* 33 (1995): 379–90.

6. Jeffrey Schwartz, *Brain Lock: Free Yourself from Obsessive-Compulsive Behavior* (New York: Regan Books, 1996).

7. Lee Baer, *The Imp of the Mind: Exploring the Silent Epidemic of Obsessive Bad Thoughts* (New York: Dutton, 2001).

8. M. Salkovskis, "Understanding and Treating Obsessive-Compulsive Disorder," *Behavior Research and Therapy* 37 (1999): 1–24.

9. Thérèse said this to one of the novices she was directing, Maria of the Trinity. Quoted in Pierre Descouvemont, *Therese of Lisieux and Marie of the Trinity* (New York: Alba House, 1993), 76.

10. Ignatius, *Saint Ignatius' Own Story*, 19.

11. Ibid., 58.

12. Sisters of the Visitation, *The Spirit of Saint Jane de Chantal As Shown By Her Letters* (London: Longmans, Green, and Co., 1922), 2.

13. *Francis de Sales, Jane de Chantal: Letters of Spiritual Direction*, Classics of Western Spirituality (New York: Paulist Press, 1988); Wendy Wright, *Bond of Perfection: Jeanne de Chantal and Francois de Sales* (New York: Paulist Press, 1985).

14. Sisters of the Visitation, *Spirit of Saint Jane*, 3.

15. Monsignor Bougaud, *St. Chantal and the Foundation of the Visitation* (New York: Benziger Brothers), 204.

16. It is notable that Saint Jane developed obsessive-compulsive disorder at a relatively late age, around thirty, and that her disorder was precipitated by the stress of the tragic death of her husband. Since late onset and acute stresses predict a good outcome, one would expect that with good therapy (or, perhaps, even with no therapy at all) such a person would do well in overcoming her disorder. But Saint Jane suffered worse and worse and worse obsessions as her life went on. It seems that the repeated advice that Saint Jane received from Saint Francis to "never consent" to evil thoughts was what fueled her obsessive-compulsive disorder.

17. John Baptist Scaramelli, SJ, *The Directorium Asceticum: Guide to the Spiritual Life* (London: Burns, Oates and Washbourne, 1924). Scaramelli devotes a hundred pages to obsessions, compulsions, and their treatment, anticipating present-day approaches. Scaramelli deals at length with compulsions. He describes mental compulsions, which he refers to as "interior acts," such as people repeating prayers and saying certain words over and over. He also describes behavioral compulsions, "exterior acts," such as people shaking their heads, pressing their hands upon their bosoms, and rolling their eyes strangely. The result of all of these, Scaramelli notes, is that "the more the thoughts are driven away the more they return to the mind." Scaramelli highlights the particular problems of endlessly repeated confessions and prayer rituals. Of the latter he notes: "Some persons are greatly distressed in reciting vocal prayers, fancying they have omitted portions, or not pronounced the words plainly, so that they repeat again and again the same words, without, of course, ever gaining any peace or satisfaction from so doing." The advice he gives is to stop the rituals: "Such people should be commanded to go forward in their prayers, and they must be forbidden ever to repeat any portion." As a result of the writings of Scaramelli and others, more people received sound counsel.

18. Theodule Rey-Mermet, *St. Alphonsus Liguori: Tireless Worker for the Most Abandoned* (Brooklyn, NY: New City Press, 1987), 195.

19. *Scrupulous Anonymous*, published monthly by the Liguorian Order of the Catholic Church, a matchless source of comfort for scrupulous Catholics (Scrupulous Anonymous, Liguori, MO 63057-9999. Telephone 1-800-325-9521).

20. C. Lopatka and S. Rachman, "Perceived Responsibility and Compulsive Checking: An Experimental Analysis" *Behavior Research and Therapy* 33 (1995): 673–84.

21. S. Rachman, "Obsessions, Responsibility and Guilt," *Behavior Research and Therapy* 31 (1993): 154.

Chapter 8: Transferring Responsibility To God

1. William James, *The Varieties of Religious Experience* (New York: New American Library, 1958), 133.

2. Monica Furlong, *Puritan's Progress* (New York: Coward, McCann and Geoghegan, 1975), 153.

3. Ida Görres, *The Hidden Face* (New York: Pantheon, 1959), 328.

4. S. T. Coleridge, quoted in Richard L. Greaves *John Bunyan* (Grand Rapids: Eerdmans, 1969) 153.

5. Jean Guitton, *The Spiritual Genius of Saint Therese of Lisieux* (Liguori, MO: Triumph Books, 1997), 15.

6. Luther, quoted in Bainton, *Here I Stand: A Life of Martin Luther* (New York: Meridian, 1995), 178.

7. Erik H. Erikson, *Young Man Luther* (New York: Norton, 1958), 265.

8. Martin Luther, *Martin Luther: Selections from His Writings*, ed. by John Dillenberger (New York: Anchor Books, 1962), xxvii.

9. Richard Marius, *Martin Luther: The Christian Between God and Death* (Cambridge, MA: Harvard University Press, 1999), 269.

10. August Nebe, *Luther as Spiritual Advisor* (Philadelphia: Lutheran Publication Society, 1894), 206.

11. Luther, quoted in Marius, *Martin Luther*, 461.

12. Marius, *Martin Luther*, 449.

13. Ibid., 304.

14. Luther, *Martin Luther: Selections*, 199.

15. Marius, *Martin Luther*, 199.

16. Ibid., 457.

17. John Dod, quoted in Roger Sharrock, *John Bunyan* (New York: St. Martin's Press, 1968), 16.

18. Bunyan, *Grace Abounding to the Chief of Sinners* (New York: Viking Penguin, 1987), 35.

19. Gordon Wakefield, *Bunyan the Christian* (London: HarperCollins, 1992), 91.

20. Bunyan, quoted in Christopher Hill, *Tinker and a Poor Man* (New York: Norton, 1988), 182. This quote is from one of Bunyan's later writings.

21. Furlong, *Puritan's Progress*, 168.

22. Ernst Bacon, *Pilgrim and a Dreamer: John Bunyan: His Life and Work* (Australia: Paternoster, 1983), 29.

23. W. R. Owens, introduction to Bunyan, *Grace Abounding*, xxi.

24. Bunyan, *Grace Abounding*, 44.

25. Marius, *Martin Luther*, 213.

26. Hans Urs von Balthasar, *Two Sisters in the Spirit*, trans. Dennis Martin (San Francisco: Ignatius, 1970), 95.

27. Thérèse, *Story of a Soul: The Autobiography of St. Therese of Lisieux*, trans. John Clark (Washington, DC: ICS Publications, 1972), 105.

28. Ibid., vii.

29. Thérèse, *Last Conversations*, 138.

30. Ibid., 129.

31. Thérèse, quoted in De Meester, *Power of Confidence*, 274.

32. Thérèse, *Last Conversations*, 139.

33. Sister Genevieve of the Holy Face, *My Sister Saint Therese* (Rockford, IL: Tan Books, paperback, 1959) 52. What Thérèse needed, in order to overcome her obsessive-compulsive disorder, was a God she could rely on, one in whom she could have complete confidence. "I need a heart burning with tenderness," she writes, "who will be my support for ever" (from the poem "To the Sacred Heart of Jesus," in *The Poetry of St. Therese of Lisieux* [Washington, DC: ICS Publications, 1996]. At the center of the relationship between Thérèse and God was the transfer of responsibility for all her sins and her fears. For Thérèse, this was the most profound understanding of what it meant to love. She expresses the idea in a poem, which reads in part:

> Living on Love is banishing every fear,
> Every memory of past faults.
> I see no imprint of my sins.
> In a moment, love has burned everything . . .
> If I fall with each passing hour,
> You come to my aid, lifting me up.
> At each moment you give me your grace
>
> "Living on Love," *Poetry of Saint Therese*, 89.

34. Heiko Oberman, *Luther: Man Between God and the Devil*, (New York: Image Books, 1992), xix; Hill, *Tinker and a Poor Man*, 73; Guy Gaucher, *The Passion of Therese of Lisieux* (New York: Crossroad, 1973), 115.

35. Jeffrey Schwartz, *Brain Lock: Free Yourself from Obsessive-Compulsive Behavior* (New York: Regan Books, 1996), 7.

36. Bunyan, quoted in Hill, *Tinker and a Poor Man*, 176.

37. Poem by Thérèse, "My Weapons," *Poetry of Saint Therese of Lisieux*, 194.

Chapter 9: A Therapy of Trust

1. I have made the point before that this therapy could work for members of other monotheistic faiths.

2. Luther, quoted in Paul Althaus, *The Theology of Martin Luther* (Philadelphia: Fortress, 1966), 449.

3. Luther, quoted in Ibid., 109.

4. Thérèse, quoted in Sister Genevieve, *My Sister Saint Therese*, 57.

5. It is somewhat of a mystery where Thérèse got the translation of Proverbs 9:4: "Whoever is a little one, let him come to me." This wording is not consistent with Bibles commonly used by the Catholic church at that time, which used "simple," rather than "little." Céline may have copied the text that way, or the Holy Spirit may have led Thérèse to remember the text as such in her reflections. The other quotes of Thérèse are consistent with the Jerusalem Bible. For a discussion, see Conrad De Meester, *Power of Confidence* (New York: Alba House, 1998), note on lx.

6. Bill Minichiello, quoted in Lee Baer, *Imp of the Mind* (New York: Dutton, 2001), 111. Fr. Minichiello is the coauthor of the authoritative text, *Obsessive-Compulsive Disorders: Practical Management* (London: Mosby, 1998).

7. This dynamic is the basic thesis in De Meester's excellent analysis of Theresian thought (*The Power of Confidence*).

8. Luther, quoted in Heiko Oberman, *Luther: Man Between God and the Devil* (New York: Image Books, 1992), 319.

9. Luther, *Luther's Works*, vol. 27 ("Galatians") 73.

10. John Bunyan, *Grace Abounding to the Chief of Sinners* (New York: Viking Penguin, 1987), 39.

11. Ibid., 19.

12. Thérèse, quoted in Guy Gaucher, *The Passion of St. Therese of Lisieux* (New York: Crossroad, 1978), 117.

13. Thérèse, *Last Conversations*, 48.

14. Thérèse, *Story of a Soul: The Autobiography of St. Therese of Lisieux*, trans. by John Clark (Washington, DC: ICS Publications, 1972), 210.

15. John Bunyan, *The Acceptable Sacrifice* (Shippensburg, PA: Destiny Image, 2001), 31.

16. Luther, quoted in Althaus, *Theology of Martin Luther*, 107.

17. Luther, quoted in Roland Bainton, *Here I Stand: A Life of Martin Luther* (New York: Meridian, paperback, 1995), 50.

18. Bunyan, *Grace Abounding*, 59.

19. Thérèse, letter to Pierre Roulland, May 9, 1897, in Thérèse, *Letters*, vol. 2, 1094.

20. Luther, quoted in Bainton, *Here I Stand*, 283.

21. Thérèse, letter to her sister Marie, September 17, 1896 in Thérèse, *Letters*, vol. 2, 999.

Epilogue

1. Paul Tillich, *A History of Christian Thought* (New York: Harper and Row, 1968), 227, 229.

2. Luther, *Martin Luther: Selections from His Writings*, ed. John Dillenberger (New York: Anchor Books, 1962), xviii.

3. Lord Macaulay, English politician, essayist, poet, and historian best known for his five-volume *History of England* (1849–61). This quote is from vol. 5. Quoted in Monica Furlong, *Puritan's Progress* (New York: Coward, McCann, and Geoghegan, 1975), 180.

4. Father Molinie, quoted in Guy Gaucher, *Story of a Life* (San Francisco: Harper, 1987), 214.

5. Pope John Paul II, quoted in Gaucher, *Story of a Life*, 217.

6. Martin Buber, *Two Types of Faith* (London: Routledge and Kegan Paul, 1951), 7.

7. Patricia O'Connor, *The Inner Life of Therese of Lisieux* (Huntington, IN: Our Sunday Visitor, 1997), 150.

Index

205